Damaged Life

D0303324

Modernization has brought material benefits to us, yet we are constantly being told how unhappy we are; crime, divorce, suicide, depression and anxiety are all on the increase too. While the process of modernization has been a major force in shaping psychology as a discipline, there is little if any debate on modernity in psychology. *Damaged Life* provides a powerful and progressive analysis of modernity's impact on the psyche. Tod Sloan highlights the effects of seemingly remote issues on all our lives showing how capitalist industrialization has had a bearing on personal experience and intimate relationships. He presents an integrated theory of the self in society, setting personality development in the context of socio-historical processes and everyday life. An alternative critical psychology is introduced which explores our understanding of and complex response to modernization.

The implications of postmodern theory are discussed and new solutions proposed to end the mass suffering of the modern self. This book should be read by all those studying or working with psychology and related disciplines such as sociology and social policy.

Tod Sloan is associate professor of psychology at the University of Tulsa, in Oklahoma, and is a leading contributor to the field of personality psychology. His previous publications include *Deciding: Self-deception in Life Choices*, London: Methuen.

Learning Resources
Centre

Critical Psychology
Series editors

John Broughton
Columbia University, New York

David Ingleby
Rijksuniversiteit, Utrecht

Valerie Walkerdine
Goldsmiths' College, London

Since the 1960s there has been widespread disaffection with traditional approaches in psychology, and talk of a 'crisis' has been endemic. At the same time, psychology has encountered influential contemporary movements such as feminism, neo-marxism, post-structuralism and post-modernism. In this climate, various forms of 'critical psychology' have developed vigorously.

Unfortunately, such work – drawing as it does on unfamiliar intellectual traditions – is often difficult to assimilate. The aim of the Critical Psychology series is to make this exciting new body of work readily accessible to students and teachers of psychology, as well as presenting the more psychological aspects of this work to a wider social scientific audience. Specially commissioned works from leading critical writers will demonstrate the relevance of their new approaches to a wide range of current social issues.

Titles in the series include:

The crisis in modern social psychology
And how to end it
Ian Parker

The psychology of the female body
Jane M. Ussher

Significant differences
Feminism in psychology
Corinne Squire

Lev Vygotsky
Revolutionary scientist
Fred Newman and Lois Holzman

The crisis of the self in the age of information
Computers, dolphins and dreams
Raymond Barglow

The mastery of reason
Cognitive development and the production of rationality
Valerie Walkerdine

Child-care and the psychology of development
Elly Singer

Rewriting the self
History, memory, narrative
Mark Freeman

Deconstructing developmental psychology
Erica Burman

Growing critical
Alternatives to developmental psychology
John R. Morss

Damaged Life

The Crisis of the Modern Psyche

Tod Sloan

London and N

First published 1996
by Routledge
11 New Fetter Lane, London EC4P 4EE

Simultaneously published in the USA and Canada
by Routledge
29 West 35th Street, New York, NY 10001

© 1996 Tod Sloan

Phototypeset in Times by Intype, London
Printed and bound in Great Britain by
Mackays of Chatham PLC, Chatham, Kent

British Library Cataloguing in Publication Data

A catalogue record for this book is available from the British Library

Library of Congress Cataloguing in Publication Data

A catalogue record for this book has been requested

ISBN 0–415–04351–4 (hbk)
ISBN 0–415–04352–2 (pbk)

Contents

Preface

The primary goals of this book are to address key issues in theorizing about the social contexts of selfhood and to do so in a manner that leads to clear implications for social action. In order to develop a general framework for the understanding of self in society, I explore the impact of modernity on the psyche. I look first at how the diverse processes of societal modernization – bureaucratization, urbanization, secularization and industrialization, for example – produce the constellation of social institutions and practices we know as modernity. Then, I describe and evaluate several perspectives that purport to explain how modernity affects us psychologically. On the basis of these critiques, the issue of modernity's impact on the psyche is reanalysed in order to define the crisis of the modern psyche. In the process, I insist on the importance of analysing personality development, everyday life, ideology and socio-historical processes as interdependent, rather than isolated, phenomena. In the conclusion, some of the practical implications of this analysis for communities, families and the larger political-economic order are examined.

Psychological and social theories tend to be abstract and often seem irrelevant. I hope to show that it is possible to use theory to understand that even though the nature of our embeddedness in society is exceedingly problematic, it is possible to formulate effective courses of action towards the reduction of unnecessary human suffering. But the attitude I will suggest in many ways runs counter to the pragmatic 'See the problem and fix it with a programme' posture that is prevalent in modern social planning. Without the sort of understanding that theory provides, many solutions are bound to be short-sighted. They may be effective in the short term, but actually work in the long run to reproduce the very conditions one hopes to change.

With regard to mainstream academic psychology, I view this book as a contribution to the project of an alternative *critical psychology*. In general, critical psychology challenges aspects of psychological perspectives that serve ideological functions, for example, individualism and reductionism.

Critical psychology also questions institutions and practices that do not foster the articulation and satisfaction of human needs and interests. As I see it, the aim of critical psychology is to expose social sources of human suffering and to suggest alternative arrangements.

To foreshadow a bit more: in these pages, I examine the widespread notion that the process of modernization has pathological psychosocial consequences. We believe we see symptoms of these consequences in crime and suicide rates, broken families, the misery of urban slums and small towns in decline, the numbers of people in therapy for depression and anxiety disorders and data from surveys reporting dissatisfaction even in the midst of material affluence.

It is obviously a complex matter to discern the actual sources of emotional strain and social chaos. In contrast to the psychological effects of modernization, the material effects of modernization are more readily visible: hospitals, electrification, administrative systems, mass communication technologies, transportation facilities. Even in the material realm, however, the actual effects of change are not always what they seem to be. For example, in the process of modernization, many societies have solved important problems in the areas of health, nutrition and the production of goods, but in each of these areas, the solutions themselves often become problems. Medical progress has made the cost of health care increasingly burdensome. Cheap foodstuffs and sedentary jobs leave members of affluent societies struggling with obesity and weight control. Careless industrial procedures have done extensive damage to the biosphere through air pollution and the dumping of toxic waste. And so on.

The exceedingly diverse *psychological* situations that might be connected to modernization are harder to catalogue than material changes. But the following questions deserve as much attention as the relations between technology and the ecosphere: Could it be that societal modernization is systematically linked to increased emotional suffering on a broad scale? Could it be that many of the material and technological achievements we glorify in the name of progress are actually producing forms of individuality that are less optimal than those that might have emerged if societal development had taken a different course? If so, could one define a set of socio-political strategies that would address effectively the problematic features of modernity?

Faced with the world's complexity, it is tempting to throw up one's hands and claim that it is all beyond human comprehension, let alone human control. Cynicism about the possibility of social transformation is rampant today, especially in academia. Rather than despair, however, we can develop forms of understanding that orient individuals and communities as they work to reduce human suffering and reverse the processes that produce what Theodor Adorno (1951) called 'damaged life'.

Acknowledgements

I wish to thank John Broughton for his patient support for this project and his excellent critical comments on various versions of the manuscript. I am grateful to my friends Peter Stromberg and Lamont Lindstrom for sharing insights from the field of cultural anthropology. Randy Earnest and Barnaby Barratt helped me think through a number of issues in psychoanalytic and critical theory. Isabel Vega deserves special thanks for consistently urging me to consider the other side of the coin on each issue. Susan Chase, Theresa Fassihi and MacAndrew Jack gave many helpful suggestions for revisions. I also wish to thank Beacon Press for permission to reproduce Figures 3.1 and 3.2 on pages 54 and 55. These were taken from *The Theory of Communicative Action*, Volume 2, by Juergen Habermas (1995).

Many of the ideas presented here were developed in conversations with seminar students at the Universidad Central de Venezuela, the University of Tulsa and the Universidad de Costa Rica. *Les agradezco a todos por su interés y solidaridad*. Financial support for some portions of this work was provided by a Fulbright research grant (1987), a summer fellowship and travel grant from the University of Tulsa (1988, 1991) and a travel grant from the Ford Foundation (1989).

I dedicate this volume to my son Daniel, now seven, whose love for life – and certain aspects of modernity – has already rekindled mine a thousand times.

Chapter 1

Damaged goods: the modern problematic

Damaged goods
Send them back
I can't work
I can't achieve
Send me back

Damaged Goods, Gang of Four
(Warner Bros 1979)

The assembly line rolls along steadily. At one end, human infants are put on a conveyor belt. They come off the line at the other end when they are adults. There is no quality inspection. If there was, the majority of these products would have to be stamped DAMAGED GOODS.

What is the problem with modernity? Why do modern societies have such a hard time producing adults capable of intimacy, work, enjoyment and ethical living? Why is it that signs of damaged life are so prevalent?

These questions are frequently framed in terms that refer less explicitly to modernity: How can I know what to do with my life? What happened to morality? Why the senseless violence? Where is the foundation for faith? Is there life beyond consumerism? Each of these questions expresses a problematic aspect of contemporary social life. Obviously, I will not be able to address all such issues comprehensively in the context of this book, but I believe the book's basic argument bears directly on a wide range of modern problems.

A feature of the modern social context is that we have become all too aware of the fact that a writer's choices are informed by ideological perspectives, worldviews and personal concerns of which they are only partly conscious. The choice of a starting point for this book, for example, could be the subject of endless debate. In approaching modernity as a topic, one could choose to privilege specific historical developments, changes in social structure, shifts in cultural systems or new lifestyles and personal experiences. Which topic deserves priority? Deliberations about where to start could fill an entire book!

To avoid falling into the quagmire of obsessive self-critique, writers can state what they know about why they make the choices they do and move on. In this spirit, I will claim that, for a psychologist, the features of modernity of greatest interest are those related directly to problematic aspects of personal experience. I will say a little about how I came to have this slant on things, for it is far from self-evident. As a specialist in personality theory and adult development, I have tried to understand how adult personalities, identities and lifestyles are influenced by experiences in childhood and youth. My research in this area (Sloan 1987) acquainted me with the everyday struggles of North Americans to make a living, get along with others, and maintain hope. Having also received training in psychotherapy, I am familiar with ways in which the machinations of the prevailing socio-economic order generate unnecessary emotional suffering at the individual level. More recently I have been working, through travel and study, to understand the psychological impact of modernization in Third World societies. In my own search to understand what is going on in these various spheres, I have found that the psychological perspectives most helpful in understanding individuals in social context fall into the category of what is known as *critical psychology*. There are as many variants of critical psychology as there are self-defined critical psychologists, but one thing they have in common is an insistence on examining the societal and cultural roots of psychological experiences that non-critical psychologists choose to view as purely psychological, merely interpersonal or primarily biological.

As an advocate for critical psychology, I attempt to link personal experience to cultural systems, social institutions and historical developments. This move is a corrective to *psychologism*, the reductive explanation of human action in terms of psychological states, but it sets up new problems. Scholarly training in psychology only rarely encourages serious attention to neighbouring social science disciplines that address other parts of the puzzle. In the case of this book, this means that some readers will perceive unarticulated spaces where a sociologist or anthropologist might find much to say. Fortunately, recent scholarly work questions the modern pretence to totality, the attempt to comprehend and encompass all that is going on. Writers are thus relieved from the pressure to present themselves as omniscient.

This said, it should be somewhat clearer why I have chosen to begin by addressing modernity at the level of everyday experience and by asking what it is that is problematic about personal experience in the context of modernity. Later in this chapter I examine ways in which modernity and its problems enter into colloquial communication and scholarly analysis. In this manner we will touch on several modes through which modernity enters everyday discourse and will note the extent to which our experience of social reality is constituted and mediated by language, culture, ideology. I have chosen, at this point, not to privilege scholarly discourse or social-scientific data on the topic of modernity. Except for the fact that bits of academic products rumble around in editorials and news broadcasts, such perspectives are often quite tangential to everyday life experience. I have also chosen to work in a speculative and anecdotal mode for a while longer before selecting a focal point. I believe scholars err in deleting from their texts much of the rumination that would actually help readers understand the author's concerns and follow later arguments. Obviously, one could proceed more systematically, but since one of my goals is to invite others to engage in theoretical work and to be patient with its zigzagging quality, I prefer not to delete all traces of my reversals and dead ends from this text. This may require extra patience on the part of the reader.

MODERN PROBLEMATICS

In everyday conversation, one often hears it said that modern life is just 'one problem after another'. Why does modern life seem so full of problems, so problematic? Let's consider a few examples. Often, problems arise because some piece of technology or social system upon which we now depend is not functioning properly for mechanical or human reasons: the car will not start, the important letter has not been delivered, the computer at the bank is broken down, the mass transit workers are on strike, or the washing machine is broken. Our routines are interrupted by such events and we feel frustrated. These few examples suffice to make us aware of the extent to which progress in our own projects is dependent on a complex network of people and machines. This new interdependence of systems of people and things is an oft commented feature of modernity. In fact, sociologists working in the tradition of Durkheim define modernity itself in terms of the increasing specialization of individual functions and the new forms of interdependence (and isolation) that follow from this.

But problems are nothing new for humanity, so could it be that there are just more of them now or that solving them matters more? Is there a new urgency that fuels the frustration we experience when things are not getting done? At first glance at least, a major problem appears to be that we are trying to do too much too fast.

Indeed, the sheer pace of modern living is another frequent topic. Urban and suburban lives are increasingly structured as a series of appointments. One finds oneself trying to squeeze in a dental appointment between work and picking up the daughter from her karate lessons, bouncing from one meeting to another, staying up late to meet a deadline the next morning. One hears, 'There is not enough time in the day!' This sentiment is often coupled with the sense that the important spheres of life, such as one's family, friends, and major projects, are neglected. In such circumstances, one is prone to long for the simpler routines of rural or small town life, preferably over a century ago. Conveniently forgetting the hardships and limitations of premodern existence, we curse modernity and imagine how pleasant it would have been to live self-sufficiently at a slower pace, with deeper relationships and more time to appreciate them.

The complexity and pace of modern living are probably related in some manner to the problems we currently face, but I would argue that the striking features one tends to notice first in surveying the landscape of modernity may be superficial ones. They are superficial in the sense that they are only the emblems of structures that produce what we see going on. One could, for example, stand in Times Square in New York City and observe that there seem to be too many people, too many cars, all making too much noise, and come to the conclusion that as a result of all this people in the scene are irritated and tense. Such an analysis would be partly correct. Studies of crowding and noise do suggest that people are upset by too much of either. My point, however, is that to leave the analysis at that level would obscure the fact that other structures operate to produce this congestion, for example, the concentration of power and money in New York City. This, in turn, is an effect of political and economic processes with a long history. So, returning to the problem of first impressions of modernity, whatever they may be (remember that pace and complexity were themes I brought up), I recommend that we should not be distracted too much by the impressive external commotion that dominates our senses.

Let me ask again, then, and try to answer at a more leisurely pace, What is the problem with modernity? What new problems, if any, do we encounter as modern individuals? I mean to ask this question as open-endedly as possible. My good friends at universities in Latin America, upon hearing me complain about one problematic aspect of moderniz-ation or another, either in my own country or theirs, would often reply, '¿Cuál es el problema?' – What's the problem? They explained their nonchalance in various ways: that change is just change, that one must go with the flow, that it is not productive to worry about things that one cannot control, and that for every negative aspect of change, there are positive aspects. Although such attitudes may reduce stress, I am still not convinced that they are justifiable, particularly if one is inclined to feel personal responsibility for general social welfare. As soon as I say this, however, I remember that feelings of social responsibility that go beyond doing one's duty within an assigned role are also an integral part of the modern worldview. It is becoming clear that before adopting any particular position of any of these issues, it will be necessary to stake out the ground for our inquiry more carefully. Note that thus far I have not specified the characteristics of a modern society; I have merely allowed myself to lean upon generally accepted usage. In the remainder of this chapter we sort through different visions of modernity in order to decide what it is that qualifies a society as Modern and we begin to see why modernity presents us with all sorts of new problems to solve.

EXPERIENCING MODERNITY

As we saw above, one quickly arrives at interesting insights by starting with what we know best: everyday life experience. By this I refer to the relatively conscious processes of understanding, perception, awareness, communication and thought that accompany an individual's daily activities. In the case of any given individual, this experience is constituted at any given moment by a unique interaction of personality, life history and social context. Ever since the nineteenth-century debates in historiography led by Dilthey (1961), it has been argued that the uniqueness of individual experience poses an immediate problem to the social scientist seeking regularities. The rich textures of individuality make it hard to perceive commonalities and make generalizations. But, if there is something about modernity that shapes everyday life experience in general and structures modern problems, might it not be reflected at least indirectly despite the diversity of modern individuality? To test this possibility, let's examine the situations of several invented, but possibly real, individuals in different parts of the world on a weekend afternoon. These vignettes are constructed to highlight certain themes, but they are based either on interviews I have done or on reports by other observers of socio-cultural trends. Anyone familiar with these situations will appreciate their verisimilitude.

> *New York:* The throbbing roar of traffic in the avenue five floors beneath his apartment competes for the young man's attention with the postpunk music on his stereo. He forces this cacophony into the background of his mental space in order to concentrate on the newspaper article he is reading. Out of the corner of his eye, he catches a glimpse on TV of a blown-out building in a war going on somewhere in the world. A friend calls and asks him out to a movie. He declines, saying he is not in the mood. After changing the radio to a classical station and turning off the TV, he feels tired and lies down for a nap. He remembers that he has to start working on a project to meet a deadline the next day. He decides to procrastinate further and begins to fantasize about the new car he would like to buy. Then, he remembers an argument he had with his boss and wonders if that will affect

his promotion. He gets up and checks the classified section of the paper to see if other jobs are available. No attractive positions are advertised. He goes to look out the window. Below, he sees a man sleeping on the pavement under a piece of cardboard and wishes he could help. He goes to get something to eat from the refrigerator. While he eats, he wonders how his sister is doing in her new job in a city hundreds of miles away.

Cairo: An adolescent makes herself up in her room for a meeting with friends at a trendy café. An image of Madonna comes to her mind as she puts on lipstick and swings her miniskirted body to the beat of the rap music video that plays on the television in the corner. She is anxious because she knows her parents will scold her as she leaves the apartment for dressing 'like a prostitute' and for neglecting her studies. Men in the street will make disgusting sounds and try to touch her. She pulls herself into a defiant stance and heads out. She feels strong and free. Later, with her friends, she watches carefully for signs that they approve of what she says and makes sure that she goes with the flow of the group. She especially hopes to impress a sharply-dressed young man who, like her, is studying to be an engineer.

Rural Venezuela: A man in his thirties sits on a stool in front of his two-room, palm-roofed house. He holds a broken bicycle chain and wonders how soon he will be able to catch a ride to town to fix it. He curses the government for promising, but not delivering, a better road and a bus service linking his farming community to the town 20 kilometres away. Without his bike, he will have to get up an hour earlier to reach the fields where he cultivates yucca and plantain in a new agricultural development project. Remembering that he had expected to own his own farm and a truck by now, he begins to feel helpless, sad, useless. His wife interrupts his worries by asking him again about money to send their 12-year-old daughter to secondary school in the capital 'to give her a chance in life'. He frowns and replies that he will have to buy himself a motorcycle first, but doubts that he will even be able to do that. His wife tells him he is both selfish and lazy as she turns back into the house. A friend stops by and invites him to the cantina for a beer. This appeals to him, but he has run out of cash and is forced to decline. His feelings of helplessness escalate.

Do these diverse vignettes capture something central about the modernity in which we are all embedded? The commonalities between them are probably not to be found in the specifics of circumstances or in the particular problems these individuals face. They each face distinct and basically unrelated sets of practical issues, but they also can be viewed as confronting problems that transcend the material realm, problems that involve an ongoing process of self-definition or self-creation in a complex social context. Their issues are not only about what to do, but also who they are and where they are going with their lives. Their identities and life projects are thus constantly reorganized in conjunction with the details of their material and social situations. Practical problems and their solutions matter to them because they are connected to a basic sense of self and related life projects. As a result, problems like not getting to work on time, arguing with one's boss, not having money to make ends meet, or resolving parental and peer pressures feel more than trivial and temporary.

But, what makes these *modern* problems in living? Throughout history, identities, life projects and practical situations have always been interwoven. In other words, the basic co-ordinates of human social existence have always been structured so as to require a degree of conscious management of who we are and where we are headed in relation to the realities we confront. In the modern world, however, all three aspects of existence seem to be simultaneously disturbed, disrupted, uncertain, or unpredictable. Furthermore, it seems that the primary forces that disturb and disrupt are traceable to the emergence of modernity itself and to our collective attempts to come to terms with it.

The situation of each of the individuals portrayed in the vignettes could be analysed in light of this perspective. The first young man's experience, integrally linked to his position in one of the hearts of modernity, appears to be characterized by a sort of chaos, a lack of groundedness, and movements in no particular direction. He seems isolated, to some extent by choice, and unable to concentrate. He has things to do, but he is not motivated. One can wonder for him: what will he be? How will he connect with others? How can he move forward if he does not have answers to these questions?

The Venezuelan's situation is somewhat different. He has practical problems to solve. These problems are set up by rapid economic modernization in his rural area. New production and infrastructural systems linking village to city have altered the landscape of economic opportunities in which he and his family must find their way. These changes indirectly implicate his identity and life projects. One can imagine that, as a man raised in a traditional peasant culture, he feels somewhat bewildered by the tasks he faces. Will he be able to take advantage of opportunities? Will he be left behind? What should he do to ensure the best life for himself and his family?

The young Egyptian finds herself at the collision point between two cultural systems, a collision set up by the forces known as modernization and complicated by the particular impact of social change on women. She probably defines her conflict simply as a difference between her own views and impulses and the behaviour favoured by her parents, but it is

one experienced by millions of youth around the globe in the late twentieth century. For all of them, their emergence into young adulthood will
be shaped to various degrees by the usual intergenerational conflict aggra-
vated by the cultural impact of global forms of mass communication
unknown to previous generations. In the case of the young Egyptian, one
may ask: How will she construct her identity out of the conflicting
elements available to her? Will she be able to centre herself? How will
she come to terms with the clash between values stemming from the
culture of family and those that follow from her scientific training?

What do we learn from these observations? I first note that my constructed descriptions of everyday experience unwittingly highlighted two
realms of living that seem to become problematic in ways I see as peculiarly modern. The first is the realm related to making a living, surviving
economically, getting ahead professionally, carrying out one's projects.
The second, not necessarily less important, is the realm of relationships
with 'significant others,' including family ties, work relations, friendships,
romantic involvements, and so forth. Throughout the rest of the book, I
will refer to these two realms as *personal projects* and *social relationships*.
These spheres of life become more strikingly differentiated from each
other under the spell of modernity and both emerge as issues for most
people only in the modern context. Only within the frame of modernity
will one find individuals for whom both personal projects and social
relationships are so consistently problematized. This problematization is
an important constituent of the crisis of the modern psyche.

TALKING ABOUT MODERNITY

These quick speculations show us that descriptions and analyses of everyday experience can lead to interesting ideas, but they leave one totally
uninformed about social and historical processes that produce the modern
context. Furthermore, as I have allowed, my speculations are themselves
conducted within a modern frame of mind. The modern frame of mind
is something one picks up in bits and pieces through processes of socialization in families, schools, peer groups and media exposure. As adults, we
continue to encounter and absorb chunks of the modern worldview in
conversations, news reports, sermons, horoscopes, textbooks and movies.
These are, of course, contrasted to or opposed by other frames of mind,
even by contrasting elements of the modern frame.

In light of this, and as a means of grounding this project in problems
that are commonly articulated by modern individuals, we take a few
snapshot looks at the ways 'ordinary people' talk about the problems
modernity poses for us. In the subsequent section we turn to scholarly
attitudes regarding the larger context of modernity and consider evidence
bearing on its nature.

Here I draw mostly on commentaries I have heard in discussions about this book project with students in courses on 'self and society' and with dozens of people in Latin America with whom I conversed about social change in their societies, but such things also get said daily as a matter of casual conversation. This is evidenced by the fact that all of my informants had a ready-made answer when I asked, 'What do you see as the main problem of modern life?' These are the most common types of responses to this question:

1 The Pace of Change: *Things are changing too fast. You just get settled into a new way of doing things and then it changes again.*
2 The Decline of Certainty and Belief: *It's hard to be certain about one's beliefs. There are so many ways of seeing the world.*
3 Unfulfilled expectations: *This is not the way I intended my life to be. I thought that by now I would have achieved so much more.*
4 The Decay of Morality: *Nobody has any morals anymore. Nobody cares for anybody else. People are just out for themselves. Why should I follow the rules?*
5 Meaninglessness: *I have trouble finding meaning in what I do. Life seems empty. I'm bored.*

Each of these responses captures a single facet of what is obviously a complex, multifaceted social process. This makes it hard to discuss one of these points without sliding into the next. To illustrate this point, I include below a commentary I wrote fairly early in this project as I was trying to weave together some of my main concerns. What I say here is not a form of discourse that I would submit for scientific scrutiny. Although many of the assertions below could be backed with social science data, their validity is not the issue now. Besides indicating the interwoven nature of the topics at hand, I also want to touch a number of chords that will be familiar to most readers to establish a common ambience of concern in connection with the modern problematic before we move on to systematic analyses.

Perhaps the most common first thought about the experience of modernity is that it is characterized by rapid change at both the individual and the social levels. Most of the people I have interviewed casually about what modernity means to them quickly think of change, progress, or development as its primary characteristics. In their minds, such change is often linked to social mobility and geographic displacement due to changes in worksites or jobs. It can also flow from shifting involvements in relationships, as evidenced in the oft-cited divorce statistics. In contrast, the premodern past is viewed, perhaps incorrectly, as a time when changes occurred slowly or not at all, when people stuck to spouse and profession for an entire lifetime. When I asked my informants if such change is a problem, they tend to say that it is not change itself that is troublesome.

In various ways they would explain that without the novelty of new jobs, new relationships and new forms of entertainment or consumer items, modern life would actually be pretty boring.

I would go on to acknowledge, however, that there might be something related to change that sets up the modern problematic. For example, the problem might be that because of change we are more likely to feel uncertain and confused. Those who are not confused and feel certain that they know what is going on are perhaps the most confused of all. There have been confusing times before, periods of great social upheaval, war and devastation. The striking thing about modern confusion is that its locus is personal identity, a confusion evidenced in each of the comments listed above. In contrast to the technological developments that rely on certainty to make things possible in the material world, modernity seems to sow only perplexity in the spiritual and psychological spheres. It is as if the doubt that Descartes proposed as the foundation for scientific knowledge returns to haunt the individual who thinks and tries to make decisions.

This perplexity is perhaps stimulated by the abundant contradictions of everyday life in industrial society. The peacefulness of the suburbs is belied by rates of domestic violence. Shopping malls overflowing with goods are frequented by people who can barely afford to live in their own homes. The lives of the destitute erupt into the lives of the better off in crime and random attacks. Our awareness of this conflict and chaos is broadened by modern communications systems. Not only do we directly experience local disintegration in families and neighbourhoods, but we are also exposed to televised images of social conflict from all around the world. Whether one watches television from the First or the Third World, a few hours watching international news coverage is sufficient to throw any sane individual into despair. But instead we mostly adapt, adjust or ignore. We learn to expect that our own moods will change at the same rate as the world around us, as if we were all on the same big roller-coaster. Whatever confusion would be appropriate in such an environment is eventually buried by pressure to keep moving along.

The pace of modernity conditions everyday experience directly, but it also makes things difficult in the realm of long-term life planning. It is hard to know what life has in store for us. As the context in which we live shifts and evolves, our lives cannot be what we intended or planned them to be. We end up living out our days in ways we never could have anticipated. The problem is not only that our lives catch us by surprise. It also lies in the probability that most of us find ourselves doing many things we do not want to do and feeling that we do very little of what we would really like to do. In the midst of a seemingly wide range of options, we often end up sliding into something we never expected.

In part, this discrepancy between preferred and actual lifestyles is due to the fact that the intentions, dreams and desires with which we were endowed as children encounter a frustrating world when we are adults. The world in which our childhood meanings were formed is no longer here for two reasons. The first is an existential reason that has little to do with social change. Our childhood perceptions (like those of adults) are not always accurate representations of the social world – they sometimes idealize the world and are also distorted by the natural limits on a child's understanding. The second reason is socio-historical. In modern times, the social world of childhood and adolescence in which our life dreams take shape is radically altered through social and technological changes by the time we become adults. The actual world that we learn about in childhood, whatever and wherever it was, will never be here again. Thus, we are prepared as youth for the 'wrong' world by elders who were not even prepared for theirs. A consequence is that our most cherished projects, nurtured as they are by childhood desires linked to once valid perspectives on opportunities, typically fall flat and do not satisfy. Those who feel this disparity to a lesser extent must have evaded the mainstream of social flux for geographical or ideological reasons and have thus been insulated from the more disruptive sorts of change.

Despite the wide availability of encyclopaedias, self-help books and other forms of published and orally communicated wisdom, most modern individuals seem to have few symbolic resources with which to comprehend the apparent chaos of social and personal life. Added to the basic irrelevance of traditional belief systems in grasping the modern situation, citizens of modern societies now experience the destabilizing, dizzying effects of relativistic education in which all beliefs appear to have equal value. One can only be certain that one's beliefs are one's own and that they are worth as much as those of the next person. Worldviews become matters of taste rather than truth. The subjective uncertainty stemming from the parallel existence of contradictory and untranslatable worldviews is often masked by the rigidity of ideological stances.

Handed down beliefs are subject to a kind of deflation to the status of mere attitudes. As their limits are discovered in the practice of everyday life, they lose their motivating power. Ideals crumble, faith withers, hope fades. One step beyond there lies perhaps the most intriguing aspect of the modern problematic: the collapse of meaning.

In the absence of systematic reflection upon the connecting threads between our everyday lives and both local and global social changes, it is certainly hard to make sense of anything, if we even bother to try. Directly linked to whatever produces obstacles to global and historical self-understanding is the trouble many of us have in finding or feeling meaning in what we do. Those of us who are not totally exhausted or cognitively constrained by the demands of survival in the contemporary world system seek antidotes for this meaninglessness. Some turn to horoscopes or to faddish new religions in search of fresh meanings to replace those which we assume must have been there once upon a time, since our grandparents and greatgrandparents at least appeared not to be struggling with such issues. We imagine that in previous eras people lived in more coherent cultural systems, total systems with fewer conflicting worldviews and few contradictions within worldviews. One's commitment to a particular worldview was so total that one would die for it, as did hundreds of thousands in the Crusades or the colonial wars. In contrast, one senses that modern individuals must pause much longer before going off to war against other systems and that key modern codewords such as 'democracy' and 'freedom' are less effective in mobilizing aggressive action. Especially in the post-Vietnam decades, their meanings have lost coherence in the wake of repeated disillusionment with actions taken on their behalf.

In attempts to restore meaning and commitment, many attempt a direct return to the once-upon-a-time by structuring their activities according to rigid traditionalism (fundamentalism) or playful weekend re-enactments of medieval tournaments. Even the impulse to revolutionary political activity can have roots in the attempt to link one's own meagre efforts in a limited situation to a larger meaning-restoring process of history. Life strategies and lifestyles are plentiful, but many individuals who have tried several of them begin to feel that there must be something more fundamental, a way of addressing the modern world which goes beyond a faddish trying-on of ways of life as if they were extensions of our wardrobes.

The question of what it is all about accounts for the turn that millions make when they look to spiritual practices or religious ideologies for answers. In these they find worldviews that locate humankind in some sort of transcendent order and offer some sense of what life is for, or at least a view of a life pattern that could be rewarding or satisfying. These usually entail reference to states beyond this life, but even if the cosmology manages to stick to what can be known through earthly perception, there is usually a transcendent order of values and ideals to which earthly events are referred. Even atheistic Marxism does this. One must wonder: Is this sense of transcendence, of a beyond, or of an ultimate purpose, an essential component of meaningfulness? Or can we discover a meaningfulness that is not chained to the need to go above and beyond our own immediate sensual, emotional and rational experience?

In a related way of framing the problem of meaning, conservative groups are fond of talking in terms of the loss of moral values. People are only out for themselves these days, they say, usually pointing at young people or corrupt politicians. According to this analysis, modern people lack all sorts of traits associated with moral virtue: perseverance, loyalty, chastity, honesty, kindness and perhaps most of all, respect for others.

The solution commonly proposed is, again, a return to traditional morality, often to a set of moral values associated with a given creed. Advocates of this solution do not seem to recognize that traditional value systems do not necessarily provide acceptable answers to modern ethical issues. Neither do they realize that the conscious return to a set of traditional attitudes and behaviours is quite different from engaging in traditional practices that have been one's own traditions from birth forward.

For some people, the problem of meaningfulness is encountered more directly at the level of everyday life than in the realm of cosmovisions. Activities begin to get repetitive. One's favourite hobbies get old. One tires of friends' usual patterns of interaction, their jokes, their anxieties, their needs. One begins naturally to wonder: what is the point of it all? What does it all lead to? Why do I have to put up with this? It may not be so bad, but it's certainly not great. Certainly not what I expected out of life. . . .

Are modern individuals as preoccupied with meaning as I have supposed? Do people really care about meaningfulness? Are they at all conscious of this as a problem in their lives? And if not, why not?

In anticipation of themes to be addressed later, I would answer that in general I do not regard conscious concern as a direct indicator of a person's motives. I am suggesting that whether people know it or not, the modern problematic revolves around the issue of meaningfulness. We glimpse the signs of this both in what people say about modern problems and in what we see people doing in order to construct meaning or find it. What we certainly do not understand very well is how meaningfulness is created or, if it is not created, why it is there from the beginning. Another way to pose this question is to wonder if there is a common experiential structure in the feeling of meaningfulness. If we had an answer to these questions, we could then ask whether something has changed that has made this common structure less effective in modern life.

The beginnings of an answer must lie in that relatively unthought space between sociality and individuality, between self and society. Strangely enough, although it is because of modernity that we even pose the question in the first place, we tend to be excluded from thinking critically within this 'psychosocial' space by modern individualistic or collectivistic ideologies or discourses. We thus mis-think the problematic, reducing society to something 'out there' that impinges on our minds, or restricting the psyche to a process 'in here' that has always been this way for us as humans (cf. Henriques *et al.* 1984).

We turn now to examine the 'out there' that is somehow 'in here' as we search for a better handle on what modernity is from the societal point of view. For such accounts, I turn to academia, a collection of sites where debate on modern society and its problems has been especially volatile.

WHAT THE SCHOLARS SAY

I have so far discussed modernity as a sort of encompassing background against which most individuals in the industrialized societies live their lives. As I have described it, this background has implicitly included features such as urban living, exposure to mass media, contact with bureaucratic work organizations, value conflicts and all sorts of other characteristics that have no necessary connection to the sort of social organization or historical period that many scholars have in mind when they use the term modernity. In other words, academic writers have tended to be much more particular in their definitions of modernity. In deciding how to examine linkages between modernity and the psyche for the purposes of this inquiry, it will be important to determine at least generally what it is that produces these forms of everyday life that appear to be radically different from life in previous eras or in non-industrialized societies.

This concern was in fact one of the key factors that gave rise to and still motivates the discipline of sociology (Haferkamp and Smelser 1992). The attempt to describe the origin and nature of modern society and its core problems characterizes the central thrust of the work of Comte, Marx, Durkheim, Weber, Simmel and Parsons, for example. In the remainder of this chapter I consider problems in defining modernity and modernization. In the next chapter I examine several analyses of the ways in which modernity may be linked to personal experience.

For scholars, the term *modernity* typically designates a loose constellation of social institutions, cultural practices and economic patterns that emerges with the advent of urban industrial economies and the democratic nation-states. It is difficult to specify the crucial features of this constellation of interwoven socio-economic trends, historical events and political developments because there has always been substantial debate and cross-disciplinary disagreement about what it is that constitutes modernity *per se*. Such disagreement makes it hard even to pin down the historical period to which modernity refers. Historians tend to locate it much earlier; for example, in certain aspects of the Renaissance. Sociologists and political theorists often link modernity to the eighteenth-century Enlightenment. Others use the term modern to refer to twentieth-century technological or socio-cultural developments, as in 'modern communications systems', 'modern aviation', 'modern art' and 'modern family life'.

Faced with this diversity, most writers on the subject of modernity first acknowledge the variety of definitions available, then proceed to narrow them down to accomplish their own purposes (e.g. Kolb 1986; Kolakowski 1990). A typical social science strategy is somewhat circular – to describe the state of modernity in terms of the factors that produce it. There tends to be a lot of overlap between such definitions of modernity. For example, Marsella (1978) describes modernity as being constituted by the following list of characteristics:

- self-sustaining growth of the economy towards increased production and consumption;
- public participation in policy agreement;
- diffusion of secular-rational norms;
- increased social and physical mobility;
- transformations of modal personality.

When all these things are happening, modernity must be there. Here the focus is clearly on dynamic change processes that characterize industrial economies and modern nation-states. For comparison, consider Etzioni-Halevy's list of the features of modernity:

- an industrialized market economy with continuous economic growth built into it;
- a proliferation of large-scale bureaucratic organizations pervading practically all spheres of life;
- a high rate of literacy and a continuous spread of formal education;
- an unprecedented reduction in inequality and growing rates of social mobility;
- a low birth-rate balanced by a low death-rate;
- urbanization;
- the declining influence of religion;
- the structural ability to absorb continuous change;
- a value system with special emphasis on universalism and achievement . . . and participatory democracy, or something very much like it.

(Etzioni-Halevy 1981: 40)

The differences between Marsella's and Etzioni-Halevy's lists are not major, but they indicate how different analytic goals lead to shifts in emphasis. Marsella is leading up to an analysis of modernization's impact on the individual, while Etzioni-Halevy is reviewing sociological models.

Partly in order to make their mark among the competing interpreters of modernity, many scholars go beyond such lists to posit an *essence* or central organizing feature of modernity. The following passage illustrates a common move:

The characteristics of modernity examined by social scientists are advanced urbanization, expanded literacy, generalized health care, rationalized work arrangements, geographic and economic mobility and the emergence of the nation-state as the most important sociopolitical unit. These are merely the surface features of modernity. The deep structure of modernity is a totalizing idea, a modern mentality that sets modern society in opposition to its own past and to those societies of the present that are premodern or un(der)developed.

(MacCannell 1976: 7–8)

In a similar manner, sociologist Hewitt argues that the essence of modernity is 'a deep sense of contrast between the organic communities that have historically sheltered (and oppressed) individuals and a new, larger world of society in which new forms of community . . . come into being' (1989: 121). Anthropologist Nash defines modernity as 'the social, cultural, and psychological framework that facilitates the application of science to the processes of production' (1984: 6). In fact, all of the best-known sociological theories of modernity attempt to reduce the complexity of the last few centuries to some core process. Weber describes the process in terms of the rationalization of social institutions. Marx discovers the essence of modernity in capitalist economic development. Durkheim focuses on the increasing complexity of the division of labour. Habermas points to the decoupling of technical systems from the cultural lifeworld. Each of these perspectives locates the emergence of modernity in different historical periods and leads to different conclusions about what, if anything, we should do about the modern condition.

Such moves to isolate an essence may indeed be valid, but only for particular analytic or rhetorical purposes. One must bear in mind the possibility that the apparent coherence of modernity as a state of social being could stem more from our own cognitive tendency to impose order on apparent chaos than from any particular inherent feature. Perhaps it is because of this tendency that most definitions of modernity do have one element in common. They emphasize the impression that, in contrast to premodern forms of society (which we choose to perceive as stable and slow to change), modernity is characterized by instability and rapid change. This feature stands out in Marshall Berman's poetic portrayal of the 'maelstrom' of changes that forged the modern world:

great discoveries in the physical sciences, changing our images of the universe and our place in it; the industrialization of production, which transforms scientific knowledge into technology, creates new human environments and destroys old ones, speeds up the whole tempo of life, generates new forms of corporate power and class struggle; immense demographic upheavals, severing millions of people from their ances-tral habitats, hurtling them halfway across the world into new lives; rapid and often cataclysmic urban growth; systems of mass communi-cation, dynamic in their development, enveloping and binding together the most diverse people and societies; increasingly powerful nation-states, bureaucratically structured and operated, constantly striving to expand their powers; mass social movements of people, and peoples, challenging their political and economic rulers, striving to gain some control over their lives; finally, bearing and driving all these people and institutions along, an ever-expanding, drastically fluctuating capitalist world market.

(Berman 1982: 16)

One could take a cue from Berman's description and decide that, rather than attempting to describe modernity as if it were a congealed endpoint, one should emphasize the *processes* of change that collectively produce the state we call modernity. Indeed, these somewhat parallel processes have often been lumped together for analytical purposes under the heading of *modernization*. But again, there is quite a bit of disagreement about which processes have had the greatest impact in the creation of modern society. The most common definition emphasizes the impact of technology by describing modernization as, for example, 'the growth and diffusion of a set of institutions rooted in the transformation of the economy by means of technology' (Berger *et al.* 1974: 15). This leads to an emphasis on industrialization as the core process of modernization, but the arguments for other points of emphasis are equally compelling. For example, might it not be that the spread of literacy is the prime moving force, as Todd (1987) argues? Or perhaps urbanization, a process that obviously predated industrialization? Or even 'delocalization', the establishment of linkages between local communities and regional, national, and international systems (Poggie and Lynch 1974: 362)? And might we not trace all these changes in the spheres of politics, economy and culture to the development of modern science, as does Marks: '[T]he rise of science has had a much greater influence on recent world history than any other single factor' (1983: 1)?

Is it possible to be more systematic in our consideration of modernity and modernization without rushing to isolate their peculiar essences? It seems that when society is conceptualized as if it were a machine with many parts, one is inclined to search for the essential source of energy for that machine. To some extent, this analytic problem is set up by difficulties in thinking dynamically and dialectically about social structure and social process.

In our analysis so far, modernity has already appeared as both structure and process. Modernization clearly denotes a process, but ends up being used to refer to enduring social structures, such as those of most Third World countries (as in 'modernizing societies'). One soon begins to be very confused about what is causing what. This problem has been addressed in the extensive literature on how societies change, another topic about which much has been said and little concluded (cf. B. Berger 1971; Eisenstadt 1973; Etzioni-Halevy 1981; Strasser 1981; Westen 1985; Haferkamp and Smelser 1992).

In view of this confusion, French sociologist Boudon (1986) claims that reality has proved all theories of social change to be failures. They appear to have either only local validity or oversimplify complex social systems. Boudon concludes that we should aim to develop perspectives that reflect the aspects of local realities that are relevant to social action. In recent scholarship, attempts to capture everything that is going on within a single conceptual framework are scorned for a number of good reasons. Apart from the fact that they may reveal imperialistic or totalitarian impulses on the part of their authors, overarching schemes tend to be structured by unacknowledged assumptions that always prove to undermine the system when it is applied. For example, if a conceptual model proposes that all modernization hinges on the development of heavy industry, how could one account for what appears to be modernization in societies that have promoted secular education, democratic process, improvements in health care, but, instead of relying on heavy industry, base their economies on small, labour-intensive rural co-operatives? To avoid such problems, I have chosen to refer to modernization as a *constellation* of processes that can come together in various arrangements of frequently occurring but not essential elements.

TOWARDS A FOOTHOLD

We still face the need to reduce the complexity of the modern social context and the processes that brought it about in order to avoid being cognitively overwhelmed. The situation can be clarified through the realization that modernization consists of many *sub*processes because different realms of society are affected by different types of change processes. Societies do not change as a whole or all at once. In a useful article, Desai (1976) demonstrates that the variety of definitions and emphases in the analysis of modernization derives, in part, from the fact that societal modernization occurs in many different social spheres. These spheres and their associated change processes are shown in Table 1.1.

As I argued in the last section, if we were to leave out any one of the elements mentioned in Table 1.1, we might still have something we would want to call modernization. In the absence of any particular element, the remaining elements could conceivably go their merry way. Industrialization can occur without democratization, for example. The spread of literacy is possible without industrialization. These elements should thus be seen as interrelated but not necessarily interdependent. Blumer (1990) demonstrates this point clearly in his attempt to show that industrialization is not necessarily the prime cause of all the ills we tend to associate

Table 1.1 Change processes associated with modernization

Sphere of society	Process of change
Intellectual	
	Growth of science
	Secularization
Economic	
	Specialization of work
	Industrialization
	Automation
Political	
	Democratization
	Bureaucratization
Ecological	
	Urbanization
	Delocalization
Cultural	
	Literacy
	Mass education
	Individualism
	Differentiation of identities
Overall system	
	Mobilization
	Compartmentalization
	Increasing flexibility

Source: Adapted from Desai (1976)

with it. Table 1.1 also suggests that unless it is possible to move to a higher level of abstraction, to isolate a form of social change that feeds into all of the subprocesses, any speculation regarding the psychological impact of modernization should link that impact to a specific subprocess and not attribute it to the whole.

Before leaving issues regarding definitions, we need to consider another very common analytic strategy, which is to define modernization as a constellation of social, economic and cultural processes related to the displacement or transformation of premodern or 'traditional' societies. This way of framing the issue relies heavily on a distinction between modern and traditional societies. Unfortunately, the nature of premodern societies is also debated, so much so that the once standard dichotomy of 'traditional' versus 'modern' social organizations is rarely invoked in contemporary cultural anthropology or sociology except to criticize it (Eisenstadt 1973). These criticisms derive from several realizations that are highly relevant to this inquiry:

1 Rather than being stable societies 'outside of history', traditional societies have histories and social processes as dynamic as those said to characterize modern societies.
2 The wide gap between modern and traditional societies is an illusion

based in part on cross-cultural contact linked to the colonial and imperial experiences of Western Europe. Upon investigation, one finds that even the most 'modern' societies are still saturated with supposedly 'traditional' social processes. All societies embody elements of 'modernity' and 'tradition' to such an extent that tradition and modernity can neither be described as dichotomous categories nor as points on a continuum.

3 The categories 'traditional' and 'modern' tend to have ideological uses; for example, to associate a description of the past with lack of innovation, boredom, conservatism, or rigidity, or to link the present with a decline of morality, lack of stability, loss of quality or chaos.

Can we conclude from these points that modernization has no essence, no central process or feature? As suggested by the third point above, the philosopher Stout argues that writers tend to focus on an essence because they have a stake in portraying modernity or modernization that way. For example, if they want to argue that science destroys traditional cultures, they will focus on science as the prime mover of modernization. If they want to prove that capitalism is the solution to our problems, they will insist that the wonders of modernity are the offspring of capitalism. Stout (1991) describes the resultant dilemma nicely:

> If I knew what modernity has been all about and what it would be to be beyond it, perhaps I would also know whether the transition beyond it had been accomplished and whether to celebrate the passing or help it along. But when writers behave as if they knew such things, and each seems to want to contradict the next, my confidence in their judgment wanes. I want to know what enables them to discern modernity's essence and issue univocal judgments about it when so many others have failed .... If, however, I claim no knowledge of modernity's essence, ... am I not reduced to silence? ... The temptation will thus be strong, therefore, to specify my topic by finding something in particular that stands for modernity itself, some set of necessary and sufficient conditions the absence of which would make a form of life pre- or postmodern, some basic trait or structural feature in terms of which modernity can be judged.
>
> (Stout 1991: 526–7)

It should now be clear why the term modernization is not as fashionable now as it was in the 1960s and 1970s. Nash (1984: 3) calls the tradition of scholarship that gave rise to the notion of modernization a 'naïve, ethnocentric, and largely erroneous paradigm'. As the term came to denote the path of 'development' which the newly industrializing societies of the 'Third World' were supposed to follow, numerous critics pointed out that the form of development proposed by the advocates of modernization was actually neo-colonialism, a guise for further Euro-American capitalist exploitation of peripheral regions. In this vein, Garnier and Lew (1984: 315) write: 'Modernization means that capitalism must finally penetrate every sphere of society. The valorization of bourgeois values (the market, profits, the firm) has become the dominant ideology and its praises are sung – or hammered out – by all the media.'

Such concerns informed my initial academic interest in the psychological impact of modernization. Having lived more than half my youth in Asia and the rest of my life in the heart of North American or European societies, I had formed two basic conclusions about the global scene: first, that most of the one billion people who live in the context of advanced modernity are not especially thrilled to be there. Second, that most of the three or four billion other inhabitants of the globe are rushing head-long towards the ideal of modernity under social and/or ecological conditions that make it unlikely they will actually enjoy the improved material standard of living they seek. The issue for me is thus as much psychological or cultural as it is economic and political. It turned out my concerns were shared by others who had studied the global situation systematically. For example, sociologist Peter Berger writes:

> I believe that the critique of modernity will be one of the great intellectual tasks of the future, be it as a comprehensive exercise or in separate parts. . . . The task is also of human and moral urgency. For what it is finally all about is the question of how we, and our children, can live in a humanly tolerable way in the world created by modernization.
>
> (Berger 1977: 111, 112)

As I demonstrate in the next chapter, the 'human and moral' aspects of modernity are often left out of academic analyses, mostly for lack of an adequate psychological framework, but also because of sticky problems in conceptualizing the links between social processes and the personal experience.

Where then do we leave the debate about the nature of modernity and modernization? If the reader will bear with me, I will take Stout's advice and resist my own urge to select an emblem of modernity on which to pin the ills I find most disturbing. The ambiguity of this chapter may be unsettling, but it will at least permit repeated consideration of numerous factors that might otherwise be eliminated prematurely.

We have seen numerous reasons why conceptual confusion exists around the concepts of modernity and modernization. To review the more important problems: The term modernity is used to refer to multiple historical time-frames. It can indicate various orders of things, for example, technological, cultural, societal, personal, economic or political. At least implicitly, the concept of modernity carries ideological baggage, in particular, Eurocentrism. The term modernization is equally problematic. It refers too globally to a diverse set of societal developments. It also contains unstated and perhaps questionable assumptions regarding the type of society that is desirable.

For the time being I retain the terms modernity and modernization to serve as a temporary foothold. Later, when the nature of my inquiry has been clarified, as well as the purposes to be fulfilled by this sort of analysis, I will argue for a more specific understanding of these terms.

The reader may be struck by the fact that, apart from the possible ideological issues touched upon, this chapter ends with a somewhat benign image of modernity. Indeed, when one focuses on modernity from an external point of view, the tendency is simply to be amazed by the whirlwind of social change and the technological accomplishments that it has produced. In the next chapter I examine the personal experience of modernity by reviewing several perspectives on the impact of modernization on individuals, particularly at the psychological level. This will help us to isolate aspects of modernization that are most relevant to understanding the crisis of the modern psyche.

Chapter 2

The psychological impact of modernization

Contentedness seems to be a scarce commodity in the storehouse of modern experience. Epidemiological studies of mental health suggest that most people who live in advanced industrial societies would affirm that in one way or another we pay a psychological price for the lifestyle we call 'modern' (Mirowsky 1989). This price is paid in different emotional currencies, depending on individual personalities and situations, such as: inability to concentrate, vague anxiety, impulses to hurt oneself or someone else, fear in the street, loss of faith, the sense that nothing is worth doing, a dullness of intellect, the desire to drug oneself, manic work habits, boredom with other people, fantasies of a radical change of lifestyle, estrangement, alienation, overdependence on the opinions of others, loneliness, depression. . . .

Attempts to define and account for the diverse crises of the modern psyche often grow into major cultural movements. In the 1940s and 1950s, existentialists such as Sartre and Camus had many convinced that their psychological anxieties, boredom and guilt were necessary attributes of human existence, merely the natural consequences of our confrontation with such existential facts as Time, Space, Death, Others and the Body. In unrecognized collusion with the modern *status quo*, they made it chic to experience *ennui* and *Angst*, feelings that were translated into various forms of dropping out in the 1960s.

In more recent decades, the psychiatric and pharmaceutical industries have teamed up to define our emotional difficulties in biomedical terms instead. Chemical remedies – both prescribed and recreational – can alter moods and thought patterns but leave individuals unenlightened about the social and personal roots of collective distress. Recent research establishing biochemical and neurological correlates of such unpleasant subjective states does not prove that processes of socialization and structures of modern life are not initially responsible for problematic experience with temperamental traits such as shyness, aggressiveness, insecurity, impulsiveness or distractibility.

Even Freudian psychoanalysis, which once promised to expose the ultimate roots of neurosis, often trips over its own ideological under-pinnings and finishes by indicting indirectly the morality of the bourgeois family when it points, for example, to the consequences of authoritarian discipline or overgratification. Furthermore, when Freud examined neur-osis and ordinary human unhappiness from a historical perspective, he found fault with civilization itself – not with the specific historical forms of social organization that construct contemporary formations of human subjectivity. As a consequence, the social contexts that stimulate the reproduction of neurosis escaped criticism from a discipline ideally posi-tioned to discern the subjective moments of the process (Jacoby 1975).

SOCIAL ROOTS OF THE CRISIS

I will now examine more systematically the claim that modernization has undesirable psychological consequences. With the support of interdis-ciplinary evidence, I will argue that many of the symptoms that are often explained away as existential, medical or 'merely psychological' can instead be traced to social roots.

We start with an overview of the claims that tend to be made about the psychological impact of modernization. These are drawn mostly from academic social science and social theory. I will not consider here the work of numerous scholars who have traced historical developments in the Western concept of the self or person (e.g. Sampson 1985; Broughton 1986; Baumeister 1987; Cushman 1990; Gergen 1991). I see this as a related and important endeavour to the extent that *concepts* of self avail-able in a given historical period must eventually enter into the experience of self in some manner. Yet such analyses are tangential to the study of the actual self. It has been relatively easy for scholars to catalogue each others' published ideas about selfhood. This practice has almost given more reality to concepts than to real people. As Broughton puts it, '[T]here is a marked tendency for the assumptions of psychology to lead to an ignorance of the concrete and historical dimensions of selfhood. Often the reality of self, what it is and what it is like to *be* one, is never even approached' (Broughton 1986: 146).

Table 2.1 lists representative claims regarding the impact of modernity on the psyche. Since I am still resisting the urge to reduce the complex processes associated with modernization to a core process, I have included statements about the psychological impact of a number of major elements of modernization, including: industrialization, urbanization, seculariz-ation, bureaucratization and economic development. This strategy will illustrate again the need for greater clarity regarding the mechanisms that are supposed to link general social processes to specific psychological effects.

Table 2.1 also shows why we need to be much more specific about which aspects of persons or personalities are actually of interest in this analysis. I have thus grouped claims about the psychological impact of modernization according to the 'level' of supposed effect.

Table 2.1 Representative claims about the psychological impact of modernization

Level of impact

Cognitive
    increased abstraction and quantification (Berger 1977)
    growth of intellectuality as a defence against urban intensification of emotional
        life (Simmel 1903)

Emotional
    insecurity (Fromm 1955)
    desexualization and increased frustration/aggression (N. Brown 1959)
    boredom (Lefebvre 1984)

Behavioural-Social
    informed, participative citizenship (Inkeles 1983)
    saturation by the multiplicity of relations (Gergen 1991)

Attitudinal
    belief in personal efficacy, open-mindedness (Inkeles 1983)
    increased capacity for empathy (Lerner 1958)

Moral
    disappearance of taboos (Kolakowski 1990)
    pluralization and relativizing of beliefs (Berger *et al.*1974)
    shift from restraint by others to self-restraint (Elias 1978)
    transformation of superego towards neurotic structures (Kardiner 1945)

Lifestyle
    conscious planning of individual life course (Berger *et al.*1974.)
    time-regimentation of life course (Kohli 1986)
    participation in multiple, unconnected relationships (Gergen 1991)
    alienated individualism (Simmel 1903)
    institutionalized individualism (Naumann and Hufner 1985)
    increased dependence on functioning of social system (Hannay and McGuinn
        1980)
    universalization of alienation and passivity (B. Brown 1973)
    self-consciousness and the 'cult of experience' (Bell 1965)

Global
    psychological distancing of self from own body and those of others (Elias
        1978)
    liberation and levelling of subjectivity, producing schizophrenia or Oedipal
        defences against it (Deleuze and Guattari 1983)
    flight from ambiguity towards univocal communication (Cahoone 1988)
    componentialization of self (Berger *et al.* 1974)
    neurosis – the splitting of experience into feeling and reason (Schneider 1975)
    subjectivization of meaning-systems (Berger 1977)

What can be made of this confusing array of trends? Each of the levels mentioned could be seen as connected to fundamental psychological processes. We are clearly not dealing with trivial aspects of personhood. While some commonality may exist among the types of change these authors associate with modernity, contradictions also exist, for example, between Lerner's idea that moderns are more empathic and the numerous others who see greater emotional distance between moderns. Such contradictions stem from focusing either on different levels of selfhood, aspects of modernization or populations.

The matter is complicated further by the fact that each dimension of change mentioned in Table 2.1 relies on a particular model of personality or selfhood – some adopt Freudian terminology, yet others think in terms of identities, roles or relationship styles. It would be convenient to gloss over these differences to offer a general statement about what the majority of these authors see going on, but too much would be lost if we were to do so. For example, if one author perceives the impact of modernity as alienation, understood in the Marxist sense as related to labour, it would be inappropriate to lump this idea with that of an author who interprets alienation to mean social isolation. The first would see political economic transformation as the goal and the second would work towards a greater sense of community.

We learn more about the complexities of the issue at hand by examining a category of writers who describe the modern personality in terms of the kind of person the modern social system *needs* or reinforces rather than in terms of what modernity is actually producing. Nash, for example, points out that modernity requires 'innovative, consciously creative persons, who are at ease with mobility and change, who are largely self-directed, and whose short-run ends are mainly economic, but whose long-run ends are achievement for the collectivity or for humanity at large' (1984: 6).

Other writers seem to know ahead of time what aspects are central, again because of their focus on what the system seems to require of us, and argue that these traits must be measured if one is to know how modernity is affecting people. For example, Black states:

> The psychological aspect of modernization has not been studied, has not been the subject of extensive research, but it has been demonstrated that modern characteristics can be measured and compared. To attempt an understanding of personality adaptation, what needs to be measured or at least evaluated is the ability of an individual to empathize with others beyond his immediate circle of acquaintances, the individual's acceptance of the desirability of change and the recognition of a need for delayed gratification in the interest of future benefits,

and the capacity of the individual to judge peers according to their performance rather than their status.

(Black 1984: 126)

Horowitz concurs that answers can be found through objective assessments of attitudes, and values:

> As the material bases of society change, human values and attitudes alter. But the question is, which attitudes change? In what direction, with what intensity, and at what rate? Will the process of industrialization elicit a concomitant process of cultural homogeneity? Will world-wide processes of urbanization and industrialization homogenize the diverse cultures of the world and produce an 'industrial man'? How will the population of diverse societies respond and adapt to the demands of industrialization and urbanization? ... An answer to these questions requires that we measure changes in attitudes of people undergoing modernization.

(Horowitz 1976: 259)

It is hard to imagine a more difficult research question for the social scientist than the one posed in these statements. Given the question, 'How has modernity affected the basic structures of the human personality?', many researchers would (and have) set out to investigate the problem in a fairly straightforward manner. How might they go about this? One strategy would be to take samples of people living in relatively 'traditional' settings in various cultures and compare them with people living in modernized sectors of the same cultures. The personalities of the subjects in the traditional and modern groups could be assessed as objectively as possible to generate profiles which could be compared statistically. Any differences observed between the groups could then be attributed to the effects of modernization. Right?

Wrong. This analytical approach has numerous drawbacks that would render findings highly ambiguous for several reasons. First, one could not know ahead of time which dimensions of personality would be relevant for such a study. If one were to use a multi-factor test of personality, one would be making the assumption that dimensions which were established in studies of modern subjects are relevant to the assessment of traditional subjects. There are no grounds for giving priority to modern arrangements of traits.

Second, the researcher would not be justified in extrapolating from contemporary traditional subjects (e.g. Nepalese or rural Bolivians in the 1990s) to reconstruct what traditional subjects of a previous century may have been like. The lives of traditional (rural, illiterate, etc.) peoples of the late twentieth century are lived out in relation to social realities that their ancestors did not experience, for example, the presence of television in the most remote villages, the literacy of their children, knowledge of city ways brought back by group members who have travelled, and so forth.

Third, it is difficult to know who should be designated as having a truly modern personality. The fact that one is living a modern lifestyle in an urban setting does not necessarily mean that one's personality development has been significantly affected by life in modern institutions. A person might, for example, stick closely to a group of others who continue to live in the 'old ways' despite being in the heart of the city. Nor could a researcher assume that mere presence in the city and years of participation in, say, factory work indicate that an individual's personality was primarily formed in the context of modern rather than traditional childhood socialization techniques. The move to the city and factory might have occurred just as the person came of working age.

These are just a few of the complicating factors that make the objective study of modernization trickier than it would seem at first glance. Faced with such problems, however, researchers could decide to proceed more carefully. They could set out a number of behavioural or attitudinal characteristics that must be present in a person in a modern setting in order to be considered truly modern and do the same to isolate truly traditional persons. They could then compare these two purified samples. They could also control for age, class, gender and subculture to ensure that observed differences could be confidently interpreted as the effects of modernization.

But wait. Something slipped past us there. The researchers themselves determined which characteristics of the person were to be considered traditional or modern. It is therefore possible that any differences they observe are simply other facets or correlates of the aspects they selected as being relevant to the modernization of the individual. Furthermore, their design does not allow them to determine what exactly it is about modernization that brought about these effects. Was it changes in child-rearing practices, patterns of schooling, secularization, or some other factor or combination of factors? Can they be sure that modernization was the primary factor in producing the observed effects? Perhaps they are picking up something that is only partially captured by their modernization dimension, for example, the impact of a specific historical or socio-cultural change such as the lifestyle and value changes associated with the impact of the Great Depression. It would be difficult to determine, for example, if the personalities of individuals socialized during the 1930s differ from those of the 1970s because of modernization effects or merely one-time historical effects.

Taking the above considerations into account, a team of anthropologists concluded a symposium on the impact of modernization with the following comments:

[T]he psychological concomitants of modernization have probably been greatly oversimplified in earlier research. It may be that the impression of a linear change of psychological characteristics from 'traditional' to 'modern' ... is more a reflection of the simplicity of research design than the simplicity of modernization.

(Poggie and Lynch 1974: 367)

In agreement with these authors, I will argue that in order to say anything intelligent about the impact of modernity on the psyche, one would have to decide what major aspect of modernity to focus on and have a good reason for doing so within a relevant sociological framework, and then, examine its impact on the most fundamental aspects of selfhood using a model of the psyche appropriate to grasping the hypothesized effects and the mediations that produce them. Let's look in more detail at a few of the major studies of the psychological impact of modernization to see how this strategy might work.

INDIVIDUAL MODERNITY

The basic question posed by sociologist Alex Inkeles is how changes in institutions and societies affect characteristics of individuals. He notes that prior to his own work only a few had studied systematically 'the process of psychosocial change and adaptation in individuals as they come increasingly into contact with modern institutions and participate in the socioeconomic and political roles characteristic of more modern societies' (Inkeles 1983: 5). Research reported by Inkeles in *Becoming Modern* (Inkeles and Smith 1974) and *Exploring Individual Modernity* (Inkeles 1983) was the first to which I turned in my search for materials on the psychological impact of modernization. But, beyond encountering a research question framed in a similar manner, I found little with which I could agree in Inkeles's approach and interpretation of findings. Because of this discrepancy and the fact that his work remains the major social psychological statement on the issue, it deserves special scrutiny.

It is important to understand the context in which Inkeles's research and similar studies arose. In the 1960s and 1970s the United States began to flex its international social science muscles along with its post-Second World War economic muscles. It was perhaps natural that social scientists who had helped smooth out wrinkles in the capitalist systems of labour and education at home would turn to address emerging concerns regarding the pace at which newly liberated, postcolonial societies in Africa and Asia, as well as industrializing Latin American countries, could be modernized without 'ill effects', i.e. socialist revolutions. Sociologists, anthropologists, and even a few psychologists began to study the determinants and consequences of Western-style modernization. Most studied macrosocial evolution in the demographic and economic spheres. Others looked at intermediate institutional changes in family structure, kinship patterns and local political institutions. Usually the aim of these studies was to generate knowledge that would in some way facilitate the process of capitalist-style modernization. In a few scattered cases, a leftist political agenda was more or less explicit in the research: the point was to demonstrate that the capitalist road to development was fraught with exploitation and suffering, hinting that socialist modes of socio-economic transformation would lead to greater self-realization and preserve a sense of community. In the case of most North American researchers of the period, however, the social projects of modernization – capitalism, democratization, individualism, secularization, and so on – were so intrinsic to the constitution of their research questions and methods, not to mention their personal belief systems, that what now appears as ideologically-motivated work in the service of capitalist modernization was able to pass as value-free, objective social science.

We see this ideological component immediately in the way Inkeles sets up his research strategy. He begins by contrasting the rural, non-industrial individual to the 'modern man'. The latter is characterized by informed, participative citizenship; a marked sense of personal efficiency; independence and autonomy in relation to traditional sources of influence, especially in personal decisions; and readiness for new experiences, open-mindedness and cognitive flexibility. These traits are contrasted to those said to characterize premodern peasant culture. Drawing on the work of Rogers (1969), Inkeles was able to portray peasant culture quite negatively, characterizing it as dominated by mutual distrust, fatalism, lack of innovation, low capacity for empathy, inability to defer gratification, etc.

One of Inkeles's primary concerns was to demonstrate that the 'progressive' traits of the modern individual make up a coherent package. He wondered whether the syndrome of the modern individual constitutes a personality type, that is, whether the group of traits he had selected hung together as a consequence of a more fundamental structure of emotions and cognitive style he called 'individual modernity'. He wanted to show that becoming modern is characterized by more than shallow attitude or role changes from which one could easily revert.

Inkeles considers this issue indirectly when he ponders various answers to the question, 'What makes people modern?' Individual modernity, he reasons first, might be the product of innate tendencies or inherited dispositions. He has no evidence bearing on the issue, but one might allow that certain inherited temperaments might be more likely to induce a person to seek the stimulation of a new life in the complex modern world. For example, an active, extroverted, gregarious temperament with low levels of emotionality could incline a person towards the exciting pace of modern lifestyles. Evidence from empirical studies has shown that each of the traits mentioned is more firmly related to temperamental factors than to environmental conditions. Nevertheless, we could assume that modernization processes are generally oblivious to individual differences of this sort. If social change processes are to have a general impact on individuals, they must be of a nature that affects the psyche regardless of how it has been fine-tuned by genetics.

Next, Inkeles considers the possibility that early family milieu is the primary determinant of individual modernity. On the basis of the generally weak empirical links between family environment and adult personality characteristics as well as a notion that 'families are more successful in endowing offspring with socio-economic status characteristics than they are in transmitting to them a set of predetermined personality characteristics' (Inkeles 1983: 17), he decides that home environment is probably less significant in the modernization process than many imagine. This conclusion, in my opinion, is a serious misstep for someone who is trying to establish that modernization affects the core of personality. Everything we know about personality structure from clinical studies tells us that early family experience is likely to be the primary factor in determining an individual's emotional and cognitive capacities for modern living as Inkeles defines them.

Continuing his search for the roots of the modern personality, Inkeles considers the possibilities that cultural factors may induce individuals to be more receptive to modernity (Weber's hypothesis) or that modern traits are adopted by imitation or cultural diffusion from the West. If either of these processes were primary, several generations would be required in order for sufficient changes to occur in socialization practices to have deep effects on personalities. Given this realization regarding the central role of socialization, Inkeles turns explicitly to neo-behaviourist 'social learning theory', the then dominant US perspective on the development of personality traits. He begins by drawing a curious parallel between Marxist thinking and the key principle of social learning theory:

> Following the leads Marx provided when he declared that one's relationship to the mode of production shapes one's consciousness, we may expect individuals to learn to be modern by incorporating within themselves principles which are embedded in the organizational practices of the institutions in which they live and work. . . . Individual modernity then becomes a quality learned by the incorporation into the self-system of certain qualities characteristic of particular institutional environments.
>
> (Inkeles 1983: 19–20)

This hypothesis guided Inkeles's research, which contrasted urban, male industrial workers in six developing societies with their rural counterparts. He interprets his data as showing that work in factories, modern bureaucracies and agricultural co-operatives 'produced significant and substantial increases in the sense of personal efficacy, in openness to new experience, and in the approval of science and technology' (Inkeles 1983: 20). Schools are seen as having equally powerful effects. Although he cannot say exactly by which mechanisms the 'incorporation' of institutional environments takes place, he decides that both school and factory have such powerful effects because they embody: common principles of organization, rational procedures for assigning power and prestige and for allocating rewards and punishment (thus rewarding initiative) and practices related to time management. He thus concludes that social learning theory would thus account for 'by far the greatest proportion of the variance explained' (ibid.). In other words, the highest statistical correlations are found between attitudes and behaviours defined as modern and variables related to exposure to factory life and modern educational institutions. This conclusion, of course, brings us nowhere nearer to knowing whether these attitudes and behaviours reflect the existence of an enduring personality structure – they might, for example, merely reflect the expression of attitudes and behaviours consistent with the temporary adoption of a modern role. In other words, the fact that a factory worker expresses more concern about punctuality and efficiency does not necessarily signal profound personality change. In shifting to a focus on intermediate institutions and an assessment of their impact through consideration of role-related attitudes and behaviours, Inkeles sidesteps the issue of whether individual modernity actually produces important personality change.

The aspect of Inkeles's study that is most troubling, however, is his conclusion that individual modernity is not associated with a decline in personal adjustment. Since he is aware of anthropological studies showing that modernization is correlated with 'deculturation, personal disorganization, alcoholism or other forms of addiction, lassitude, depression, anxiety, hyperaggressivity, and evidence of stress' (ibid.: 20–21), he initially chooses not to make up his mind on this issue until he has more data. The data he collects lead him to conclude that 'in general, there were no consistent differences in the psychic adjustment of those who were more exposed to factory work, urban living, or the mass media. . . . [T]he urbanized, industrially employed ex-migrant tends to be no worse off psychically than his cousin who stayed on the farm' (ibid.: 21).

Let's look more closely at the steps that lead Inkeles to his conclusion that mental health is not adversely affected by modernization. In a chapter called 'Personal adjustment and modernization' he describes his efforts to 'salvage the hypothesis that factory work and urban life are detrimental' (ibid.: 273). Unfortunately, his choice of an instrument to assess mental health may have made it impossible for him to detect trends that might have supported this hypothesis. As he acknowledges, the choice of a cross-culturally valid measure of personal adjustment is complicated.

For practical reasons, he was forced to reject full psychiatric assessments. He thus developed the Psychosomatic Symptom Test as his basic measure of 'personal adjustment' and found no significant associations with individual modernity, except in India, where a decrease in symptoms was noted. He concluded: 'We found no basis for asserting that individuals more exposed to modernizing experiences, or who were more modern in attitudes, values, and behaviour, were less well-adjusted than those whose modernity was less advanced' (Inkeles 1983: 274). Further on, he writes: 'Our data ... decidedly challenge that idea that individuals, *merely because they live in cities and work in industry*, are less well-adjusted than those living in the countryside and working on farms' (ibid.: 277).

Core items on the Psychosomatic Symptom Test of personal adjustment included troubled sleeping, nervousness, shortness of breath, headaches and bothersome dreams. The concurrent validity of the scale was established in part by the fact that responses to these items tended to be correlated with the expression of dissatisfaction and negative sentiments. It is this observation that cued me into the problem of basing conclusions about mental health and modernization on a psychosomatic symptoms test.

Even at the time of Inkeles's research in the 1960s, the consensus among psychiatrists was that psychosomatic symptoms stem from 'chronic attitudes or long-continued insufficiency of affective discharge' (Hinsie and Campbell 1970). In Freudian circles they were understood as the product of intra-psychic conflict related to the repression of unacceptable impulses. What we do not know is whether modernization tends to affect personality structures in such a way that psychosomatic symptoms are more or less likely. Modernizing influences might alter the structures that regulate the production of somatic systems. For example, certain psychodynamic theories regarding the impact of modernization (e.g. Kardiner 1945; Westen 1985) hold that the typical individual's superego is altered in a manner that reduces the capacity for repression. The reduced incidence of repression-related neurotic symptoms, such as hysterical conversion reactions, in European and North American populations over the last century seems to support this hypothesis. It is quite possible that what used to be repressed is now 'acted out', leading to decreased evidence of psychosomatic symptoms. If this were so, the more modern subjects would definitely appear healthier on Inkeles's primary measure of adjustment, but might in fact be poorly adjusted in other ways.

One could also entertain an opposing hypothesis. Certain cultural aspects of modernization unrelated to industrial work might lead to increased self-understanding and better interpersonal communication about complex emotions or even better recognition and understanding of somatic symptoms. Inkeles acknowledges this possibility when he discusses the impact of education on adjustment. Such awareness on the part of workers could offset the stress of industrial work and thus reduce levels of psychosomatic symptoms. It might also lead them to seek medical attention sooner. In short, the Psychosomatic Symptom Test itself may be so highly correlated with the psychic state of individual modernity that it does not constitute an independent measure of adjustment.

In my opinion, the consequences of this methodological decision are serious. It not only allows Inkeles to abandon a search for negative consequences of modernization – for example, the possibility that subjection to the regimen of factory life might be equally damaging to mental health as work on the farm – it also sets him up to be an apologist for capitalist industrialization. This is especially clear when he analyses the benefits of industrial life in terms of windfall profits for society:

> [T]he main business of the factory is to manufacture goods, and the changes it brings about in men ... are produced at virtually zero marginal cost. The personality changes in men stimulated by the factory are therefore a kind of windfall profit to a society undergoing the modernization process.
>
> (Inkeles 1983: 105)

As we saw earlier, Inkeles is able to maintain the idea that modernization effects are benign because he separates modern institutions from the social disorganization associated with their establishment. He can thus assert that city life and industrial work are not to blame for the psychic malaise of the modern individual: '[M]odernizing institutions, per se, do not lead to greater psychic stress. We leave open the question whether the process of societal modernization in general increases social disorganization and then increases psychic tension for those experiencing such disorganization' (ibid.: 114). A few of the questions that need to be asked of Inkeles when he offers such internally contradictory statements are: What is the driving force behind the urbanization and industrialization? Why is massive social disorganization tolerated in order to foster these processes? Why have Western social scientists gone to such lengths to dissociate industrialization from its ill effects?

INDUSTRIALIZATION: THE ROOT OF ALL EVIL?

As we have noted, the processes associated with modernization are interwoven in such a complex manner that it is very difficult to sort out what is influencing what. Clarity is equally elusive when we consider the influences of subprocesses of modernization such as the spread of literacy, democratization, or secularization.

A posthumously published book by the influential sociologist Herbert Blumer, *Industrialization as an Agent of Social Change* (1990), tackled this analytic problem by examining arguments that attribute various ills to industrialization. The lessons of Blumer's critique merit discussion because industrialization is a good candidate for consideration as the central defining feature of modernity. Also, if one wishes to attribute negative psychological effects to any aspect of modernization, many of Blumer's principles must be taken into account.

In its essence, what is industrialization? Blumer answers: a mode of production involving the manufacture of goods with the use of machines. This mode of production necessarily includes mechanization, systems for procuring raw materials and for distributing goods, and other services related to the production system.

It is often supposed that industrialization is the prime mover behind the various social problems that emerged simultaneously with the industrial revolution. Blumer reviews the now familiar list: disorganization, stress, disorder, discontent, alienation, dislocation, congestion, overcrowding, family breakdown, labour agitation. In typical analyses, industrialization is seen as the principal causal agent of these disruptions, but Blumer argues that industrialization, in and of itself, has no necessary consequences. His analysis shows that the nature and extent of the impact of industrialization actually depends entirely on the interaction of the pre-existing context with specific features of the type of industrialization that occurs. Among the contextual factors that mediate the impact of industrialization, Blumer (1990: 58–75) mentions the following, each of which can be shown to have no necessary structure or impact:

1 *The structure of new positions and occupations*
   These vary widely depending on the type of industry, policies, community ideologies, existing labour practices, worker attitudes towards the new positions.
2 *The apparatus for filling positions*
   Methods for attracting, recruiting, selecting and allocating workers determine, for example, the extent of mingling of ethnic groups in the newly-formed work-forces.
3 *The new ecological arrangement*
   The location of the factory is neither necessarily urban nor aesthetically unpleasant.
4 *The regimen of industrial work*
   It is usually assumed that a new regimen, often boring and difficult, provokes protest and discontentment, but these are not necessary conditions – the work could be organized differently.
5 *The new structure of social relations*
   New groups are created and these begin to establish relations with pre-existing groups with results depending on types of interaction.

6 *New interests and interest groups*
There is no way to predict whether new groups will be nationalistic, trade-oriented, ethnic, etc.

7 *Monetary and contractual relations*
Whether these are exploitative depends on the type of relations that are established.

8 *Goods produced by the manufacturing process*
These can lead to new patterns of consumption and associated lifestyles that affect public and family life, but with no uniform impact.

9 *Patterns of income*
In general, increases in per capita income occur, but this has no necessary effect because of different sorts of distribution and investment.

A set of changes such as these can, of course, stimulate a great deal of reordering in social life, but Blumer emphasizes that in each specific case of change no particular consequence can be said to follow as a matter of course.

Blumer's point is thus that it is irrational to continue to allege that industrialization is the cause of social disorder because it forces people to adjust to a new framework, destroys the traditional order of values and customs, and creates expectations for a higher standard of living. Industrialization is wrongly blamed for the various consequences of these changes, which include '(a) a variety of disturbed feelings or psychological disorders, (b) a disruption of groups and institutions, and (c) a variety of more or less violent expressions of protest' (Blumer 1990: 105). In category (a), our present concern, Blumer lists anxiety, hostility, anomie, unrest, rebelliousness, and loss of purpose among the supposed direct psychological consequences of the changes prompted by industrialization. He does admit that these are certainly among the states of mind associated with changes that might coexist with processes of industrialization, but he asserts again and again that other reactions are equally possible because individuals and groups related to the industrialization process take up different stances towards it and are affected by it differently:

> [A]ny careful inspection of what takes place in instances of early industrialization reveals that there are different ways in which traditional life is affected . . . : rejective, disjunctive, assimilative, supportive, and disruptive. . . . Usually, different parts of the traditional order respond simultaneously in different ways to the entry of industrialization. . . . The industrializing process is neutral and indifferent to the different ways in which these parts answer. Industrialization provides the occasion and sets the stage for changes in the traditional order; it does not determine or explain what takes place in that traditional order.
>
> (Blumer 1990: 101–102)

Blumer therefore concludes that there is nothing in the essence of industrialization that necessarily produces social disorder or psychological problems. To some readers this will seem preposterous: How could anyone familiar with the historical record of exploitation and misery associated with industrial development put forward such an argument seriously?

Blumer's answer comes when he provides his own account of the factors that produce the social disorganization that seems to coincide with industrialization. He sees industrialization as just one part of a much broader form of contact between types of worlds or cultures. Stable, traditional orders are disrupted when awareness of the new world of possibilities stirs up human desire. This new world of 'modernizing influences' arrives by means of books, travel, ideas, foreign products, etc. This collage of influences

> may lead people to develop wishes for new comforts, standards of a higher level of living, wishes for higher wages, a desire for the education of children, a demand for adequate public and social services, a wish to exercise control over conditions of work, a wish to improve one's social status, a desire to have the rights enjoyed by similar groups abroad, and a favorable regard for imported political and social doctrines that offer prospects of a better life.
>
> (Blumer 1990: 116)

Repeatedly, Blumer's point is that the simple fact of mechanization for the production of goods occurs in a variety of individual and group contexts that determine the way such processes will affect society as a whole. Before I evaluate Blumer's position, consider this summary of his argument:

> Thus, in the case of early industrialization, disorganization does not exist in the removal of productive functions from the family, or in the separation of the nuclear family from the extended family, or in migration to congested urban areas, or in unsatisfactory conditions of work, or in severing individuals from a paternalistic or feudal system, or in differences between labor and management, or in the rise of new sets of wishes and aspirations. These may set occasions for disorganization but are not its substance. Instead, whether or not disorganization occurs depends on how the family deals with the removal of its productive functions, how the nuclear family mobilizes itself when removed from the extended family, how migrants work out adjustments to urban living, [etc.] . . . The 'how' of each of these instances is not given by the particular situation that sets the need for action. Its explanation must be sought elsewhere, predominantly in the state of the resources that allow for the mobilization of action.
>
> (Blumer 1990: 119)

I consider Blumer's analysis especially useful because it highlights the need for extreme caution in the analysis of social change. Nevertheless, it has a disturbing flaw. This flaw stems not from Blumer's reasoning, which appears to me quite satisfactory, but from the project in which the entire analysis is couched. In his attempt to teach sociologists how to think better about social change, he loses track of the moral and historical function of social analysis. In my opinion, which I hope to justify in this book, he could easily have avoided this trap if, instead of stopping with his point about how to reason about social change, he had added comments to this effect: The fact that industrialization does not necessarily lead to any of the social ills that often coincide with it makes it all the more reprehensible that the individuals and social classes that developed and profited from the industrial system did not choose to establish less exploitative systems and show more concern for the people whose labour power contributed to their enrichment.

In short, Blumer sidesteps the fact that the forms of industrialization that we have known in the West have been primarily defined by capitalist modes of operation, with all of the attendant attempts to divide the working class, destroy solidarity and community, produce dependency, and concentrate power in the hands of the owners of the means of production. Of course, as Blumer argues, things might have been different, but, in most cases, they were not. His analytical efforts would have been better placed if he had analysed why, in the presence of objective opportunities to improve general well-being in very important ways, the capitalist class has historically done only the minimum necessary to help the working classes subsist and produce a new generation of fit workers.

MODERNIZATION AND CONSCIOUSNESS

Prominent among the less empirical, but more theoretically sophisticated studies of the impact of modernization is *The Homeless Mind: Modernization and Consciousness* (Berger *et al.* 1974). The senior author, Peter Berger, is well known for his contribution to the sociology of knowledge in *The Social Construction of Reality* (Berger and Luckmann 1966). His general orientation could be described as *phenomenological* in that he privileges the actor's subjective interpretations of reality in analyses of social behaviour. Ideas and values are emphasized as determinants of individual behaviour, while social structures and economic processes drop into the background. *The Homeless Mind* could be seen as an exercise in linking the macrosocial structures of modernity to modern consciousness. The issue is more than academic, however. The authors acknowledge early on that they are concerned about the potentially disruptive effects of modernization and economic development. In the passage below the question is put rather strangely, in fact, because they were writing at a time when the failures of 1950s and 1960s Third World modernization schemes were starting to become apparent.

> We believe that the most important question facing anyone responsible for 'development' is, 'How much suffering is acceptable to achieve certain economic goals?' There are regimes (incidentally, both capitalist and socialist ones) that are prepared to sacrifice an entire generation or more. There are others (again, both capitalist and socialist ones) that try, as far as they can, to minimize the human costs of each step in the process.
>
> (Berger *et al.* 1974: 7)

In order to address this issue, the authors present an elaborate descriptive account of the psychological impact of modernization on consciousness. By modernization, Berger and his colleagues refer to 'the institutional concomitants of technologically induced economic growth' or 'the growth and diffusion of a set of institutions rooted in the transformation of the economy by means of technology' (ibid.: 9). This definition is useful because it reduces the clutter of other definitions without losing comprehensiveness. It embodies a distinction between primary and secondary 'carriers' of modernization such as bureaucracy on the one hand and urban living on the other. By consciousness, the authors imply roughly what I described in Chapter 1 as personal experience and modes of understanding in everyday life.

The ensuing analysis of the impact of modernization on consciousness examines three major modes of impact: participation in technological production, the experience of bureaucratic processes, and the pluralization of lifeworlds. In each case, various lifestyle and cognitive effects are noted.

How are individuals engaged in technological production affected by their work? Berger and his colleagues state that such individuals sense that they work within a horizon of potentially available scientific and technical knowledge carried by experts. Workers themselves know that they are replaceable and transferable parts of a mechanistic process. They have some understanding of where they fit into a production sequence and that their participation and production in general can be assessed quantitatively.

The authors of *The Homeless Mind* hypothesize that certain cognitive styles could develop as a consequence of extensive experience in such a setting. For example, one might begin to see reality as a set of interdependent components or separable units or one could begin to see means as analytically separable from ends. Similarly, one would begin to separate work from private life and a person's organizational function from feelings towards that person. Under such conditions the worker aspect of self could be isolated from the private aspect of self. One might even begin to tinker inventively with the private self just as one must tinker to get something running again at work. At work, however, the emotional self must be suppressed in order to function as a cool and controlled part of the machine. The authors point out that this could produce a 'cleavage in the emotional economy of the individual' that may produce anxiety and 'even more severe psychological disturbance'. A certain amount of both internal and external 'emotional management' becomes necessary.

In contrast to Inkeles, Berger and his colleagues express some concern about the forms of psychopathology that might arise in the industrial context, but are more interested, it seems to me, in showing that the cognitive style necessary for industrial work spreads through society via secondary carriers such as schools and the mass media.

In their analysis of the influence of bureaucratic processes, the second hypothesized mode of impact, we find a similar move. In the experience of bureaucratically organized institutions one learns that each person has a limited competence and function, that proper procedures must be followed, that anonymity of client and bureaucrat are essential to the fair functioning of the institution, and so forth. This experience fosters a cognitive style characterized by an interest in orderliness and organization, the expectation of predictability and justice, the control of emotion according to role requirements, and the acceptance of the place assigned to one by the bureaucracy. Since these cognitive styles carry over into private life as well, one finds bureaucratic procedures for making family decisions, carrying out chores, resolving disputes among playmates, and so on. Berger and his colleagues conclude that bureaucracy's primary impact involves the establishment of connections between the individual and the larger society. In practice this means extensive contact with strangers and encounters with modes of thinking that are unfamiliar.

The third mode of impact on consciousness is related to this last point. As institutions related to technological production and bureaucratic power expand, multiple new social spheres are created. Not only is home life increasingly separated from work life, but other zones of activity open up which may have little to do with each other – clubs, hobbies, religious groups, sports. This 'plurality of lifeworlds' replaces the traditional integration between life experience and spiritual worldviews. A certain segmentation or fragmentation occurs, forcing individuals to attempt a 'multi-relational synchronization' of their different activities, to organize these into a life plan (a 'career'), and to develop, in general, a modern identity. This identity is characterized as peculiarly open, differentiated, reflective and individuated. These characteristics, combined with the secularization that accompanies the pluralization of lifeworlds, sets up the modern person for a 'permanent identity crisis, a condition conducive to considerable nervousness' (Berger et al. 1974: 78). In this context, Berger *et al.* posit that as a result of modernization individuals have lost their metaphysical homes and entered into a condition of homelessness. The remainder of their book examines various reactions to this condition and the possibilities for more satisfying solutions at both the personal and social levels.

The analysis of the psychological impact of modernization presented in *The Homeless Mind* is impressive both in its scope and its relevance for everyday life. Its strongest point is that it traces specific psychological effects to specific forms of participation in modern institutions. For example, instead of arguing that science destroys personal belief and thus provokes a loss of meaning, we learn that everyday experience in school or work requires the sorts of cognitive abstraction and contact with other belief systems that relativize religious traditions and might lead one to call beliefs into question and evaluate them on scientific grounds.

In my view the main problem with the analysis presented in *The Homeless Mind* is its assumption that most of the 'action' in the relation between modernization and consciousness occurs in the interaction between the subjective awareness of adults and their immediate situations. This reduction of the sphere of analysis to cognitions or interpretations operating in situations is characteristic of phenomenological sociology and symbolic interactionism as well as social psychology. Berger and his colleagues occasionally express awareness of two other dimensions – socialization and political-economic structures – that are part of the big picture, but they play down these in order to focus on the surface features of social behaviour. This oversight occurs when they discuss nervousness, psychological disturbance, or identity crises as reactions to modern life-styles without examining the possibility that the personalities of modern individuals are already different because of modern childrearing practices. It also occurs when both bureaucratic procedures and industrial work are separated from the political and economic contexts in which they arise. This leaves it unclear, for example, whether the cognitive styles engendered by factory work in early capitalism would be different from those induced by participatory work teams in, say, Swedish factories.

In summary, I would argue that Berger and his colleagues missed a chance to critique modern institutions for their impact beyond cognitive and lifestyle effects. This allows them to present the issue of the impact of modernization as an interesting academic study of self and society and to minimize the urgency of understanding and addressing the profound levels of suffering that follow in modernity's wake.

THE PRODUCTION OF NEUROSIS

We now examine an important approach coming from a direction opposite to Inkeles and Berger, one that begins with a critical posture towards capitalist industrialization and attempts to link it directly to the formation of psychopathology. Most analyses of this genre draw on both Marxism and psychoanalysis to make their case. They also tend to be heavy on theory and light on empirical verification. This is due in part to the fact that both ideological and unconscious processes are not easily observable, except through their hypothesized effects. One is left having to judge the merits of the analysis by its degree of correlation with what one already knows on the basis of other observations, the historical record, or personal experience.

Perhaps the most extensive and detailed Marxist-Freudian account of how the rise of capitalism has affected personality structure is to be found in Michael Schneider's *Neurosis and Civilization* (1975). The bulk of Schneider's argument rests on basic Marxist socio-economic concepts which we can only review briefly here (cf. Bottomore 1983). In particular, the advance of capitalism is seen as relying on the increasing substitution of 'exchange value' for 'use value'. In this process the leading motive for production shifts from production for use and the direct satisfaction of needs through simple trade to the production of commodities for exchange. In the latter mode, a product's value is determined by its worth in money, perhaps quite independently of its possible usefulness. As a consequence, the immediate satisfaction of needs takes second seat to the accumulation of values that can be exchanged. Any useful product becomes merely an intermediate step between quantities of 'capital'. The labour expended in the creation of a product can then be considered abstractly according to the average amount of time needed to produce it. The particular creative capacities of the individuals who make the product become irrelevant; in fact, they are forgotten for purposes of standardization. Marx's famous but widely misunderstood notion of *alienation* was developed to describe this process.

Under the capitalist organization of work, the life of the workers – their creative activity – enters the product, but they cannot see themselves in it. They have not chosen freely to make that particular product. They merely sold their labour power and time to the capitalist. Alienation therefore refers to the estrangement of workers from control over their own life activity. Given this general starting point, Schneider attempts to show more specifically how the rise of capitalist wage labour and the attendant condition of alienation have changed personality structures.

Pre-capitalist social relations, according to Schneider, were

> mythologically and religiously embellished master–servant relationships; but it was not yet – as in capitalist society – a case of objectified but of personal dependence relationships in which the social-instinctual and emotional structure was also embedded.

(Schneider 1975: 129)

In the objectified relationships of capitalist society, money becomes the purpose of work. Concrete needs are fulfilled through the attainment of money rather than through direct action designed to satisfy needs by, for example, hunting, farming, building, etc. Schneider lists a number of ways in which this social transformation may have affected the general form of the psyche. Unfortunately, the specific mechanisms by which these psychological changes are supposed to have occurred are not always explicitly described. He claims, for example, that the primacy of money led to increased lust and insatiability. The 'boundlessness of exchange value' destroyed the promise of full gratification and concrete satisfaction. Instincts, since they are connected to real satisfaction, are further and further denied in the pursuit of wealth.

These descriptions, one assumes, apply mostly to the rising capitalist class. According to Schneider, the basic personality structure of that class functions in terms of its retentive and regulative aims – what Freud described as the anal character and mistakenly traced largely to the intrafamilial management of anal-stage hostility towards parental control. Leaning on the Weberian thesis, Schneider widens the Freudian scope of analysis and argues that Protestantism served an important function in shifting emphasis from oral gratification to anal control. Displacing the emotionality and expressivity of Catholicism, Protestantism provided a religious practice that induced 'increasing inwardness, desexualization, suppression of the senses, and abstraction' (Schneider 1975: 136). Simultaneously, the Protestant religious movement achieved a 'transformation of aggression against the new capitalist masters into moral and religious guilt feelings which constitute the social compulsive character capable of supporting the accumulation of capital' (ibid.). The growing demands of production required a form of inner work-compulsion to accomplish what external force had done before. Schneider postulates that in this process individual capitalists and middle-class emulators began to lose their capacity for surrender, pleasure and intoxication (oral capacities) and instead demonstrated more ego control: decision, determination, watchfulness. Capacities to let oneself go, to relax and enjoy, were systematically devalued. Only after achieving a certain accumulation of capital could the fruits of one's self-control be enjoyed through luxuries, but this enjoyment was plagued by conflict. The desire for further accumulation battled against desire for enjoyment. (The modern solution to this dilemma seems to be the tax-deductible business luncheon!)

And the working class? Workers were not, in Schneider's analysis, affected immediately. Subsistence wages prevented accumulation. It was probably not until the bourgeoisie gained political power and imposed more and longer workdays that the socialization practices of the working class changed accordingly. Parents began to suppress their children's 'polymorphous perversity' as a preparation for factory life (which in the nineteenth century often began at age 7) and imposed rigid notions of orderliness and cleanliness in imitation of bourgeois standards for proper conduct.

For Schneider, then, a primary effect of the imposition of capitalist rationality (with the aid of Protestantism) was the division of experience into two realms: feeling and reason, id and ego. These realms have existed as experientially separate at least since the Greeks, but capitalist social relations reduced the level of free play between them. Thought would serve as the master of passion to the extent that certain fantasies or wishes would be totally blocked from consciousness. *Repression* became a common defence mechanism for those who had to maintain complete denial of their sensual needs. The failures of repression – what nineteenth-century psychiatrists began to catalogue as the *neuroses* – could thus be interpreted as indirect protests against capital's attempt to pay with cash the compensation for instinctual denial.

On the surface this argument may seem far-fetched. Its validity can only be tested by examining the connections Schneider proposes as mediating institutions between capitalism and mental illness. In lengthy chapters he examines three spheres: family relations, the capitalist organization of work and commodity consumption. I summarize his propositions here.

Family relations: With the advent of capitalism, various changes in the feudal mode of production (in particular, the separation of the domestic sphere from the sphere of production) upset the system of patriarchal monogamy on which the inheritance of private property was based, unleashing a chain of effects: family insecurity, adultery, and new forms of prostitution. The 'family' soon became an ideal to be achieved, not the reality. Further weakening of patriarchal authority followed the agglomeration of capital in larger impersonal organizations, with the consequence that the new political and commercial autonomy of the bourgeois class crumbled into 'ego weakness', a symptom of a degraded social position.

Capitalist organization of work: In the phase of monopoly capitalism, a social atmosphere of compulsion and satiated idleness was created. Work had previously been a shield against neurosis. Mass unemployment for the working class and the idleness of the bourgeois stockholder both created conditions for neurotic illness. Nervous strain became even more prevalent with the deskilling of work, the introduction of shift work, isolation from other workers, reduced upward mobility, and the reduction of responsibility to mere supervision of multiple automated machines. Among the consequences for the working class are drug addiction, alcoholism, malingering, sabotage, psychosomatic illness and physical exhaustion.

Commodity consumption: Especially among the youth in capitalist society, the reality principle of compulsory work is 'camouflaged by the capitalistically perverted "pleasure principle" of a totally unfettered mania for buying' (Schneider 1975: 214). A sort of commodity psychosis sets up a harmony between an ego that represents the offerings of capitalist society and an id that desires them.

What are we to make of Schneider's account? The fact that it is not buttressed by evidence at certain essential points is not the primary problem with his approach. I would argue instead that besides succumbing much too often to sweeping generalizations across centuries and social classes, insufficient attention is given to the specific mechanisms through which neuroses might be created by capitalist modernization. Neuroses depend on complex and varied structures of personality. They could, in fact, be triggered by the three spheres of society analysed by Schneider, but we need to know much more about how, for example, the decline of patriarchal authority in a specific generation changed socialization practices experienced by the next generation in such a way that forms of neurosis actually evolved.

Wexler (1983) points out that Freudo-Marxist analyses have often failed in part because they neglect to demonstrate how the reproduction and transformation of capitalist social relations occurs at the level of concrete social interaction. They have tended to ignore that zone of life so obsessively documented by liberal social and personality psychology under the rubrics of interpersonal attraction, person perception, small group process, attitude change, etc. The hypothesized effects of capitalist social relations on personality development may actually occur, but the complex relationships that produce them need to be spelled out if associated critiques are to be compelling.

Furthermore, in his rush to critique capitalist social relations, Schneider fails to consider the possibility that individuals with different personality structures or from different subcultural backgrounds may have dissimilar reactions to the pressure of advertising or to the monotony of the assembly line. The isolated variants and anomalies in the supposedly hegemonic process of capitalist social reproduction often mark the loci for possible transformation: work slowdowns and absenteeism, people who choose to live with fewer gadgets, young men and women who attempt to preserve community life, etc. A critical psychological analysis must take into account the various forms of individuality that exist despite the apparently overwhelming character of an oppressive ideological structure or form of social organization.

Schneider also relies on an unnecesarily mechanical interpretation of Freudian concepts and fails to show that the unconscious structures he cites are more than metaphorically parallel to the behaviours he tries to link to capitalism. For example, in the absence of further analyses of such linkages, one must wonder, Is it really an oral fixation that stimulates consumerism? An anal personality that results from Protestantism or repetitive factory work?

Much more could be said about the curious hypotheses that emerge from the blending of Marxism and psychoanalysis. Some argue that such a synthesis is possible and indeed necessary if we are to account satisfactorily for social behaviour (Lichtman 1982; Kovel 1981). Certain Marxists would prefer to keep psychoanalytic theory at a respectful distance (Tolman and Maiers 1991; Tolman 1994). Meanwhile, most Freudians seem content to operate without assimilating the political and economic constructs that Marxism supplies.

The specifics of these debates cannot be entered into at this point, for there remains the more general issue of how to conceptualize adequately the aspects of the social order and of social change that play a part in the crisis of the contemporary psyche. In other words, we have yet to settle on a general framework for understanding the process of modernization and the means by which it might set up the crisis of the modern psyche. The articulation of such frameworks is the task of Chapters 3 and 4.

Chapter 3

The colonization of the lifeworld

Soon after embarking on a review of the extensive literature on modernization, one notices that the scholars, social planners and politicians who
write on the topic have generally adopted stances either in favour of
modernization or against it. For purposes of comparison, I will refer to
these polar positions as the *affirmative* and the *critical* perspectives. Few
people with opinions on the matter would fall completely into one camp
or the other, but the two perspectives nevertheless operate powerfully at
the level of what phenomenological philosophers call *foreunderstandings*.
Such foreunderstandings operate as biases that influence decisions about
what factors are relevant when evaluating modernization's impact. Not
only do they incline one to focus only on particular facets of modernization – political, economic, socio-cultural – but they also include judgements about what *should* be occurring in the sphere under consideration
– e.g. democratization, privatization, secularization. Moreover, as we saw
in Chapter 2, such foreunderstandings also determine the extent to which
the psychological impact of modernization is a relevant consideration. To
prepare the ground for an explanation of my own position on this matter,
I will outline the two perspectives and briefly examine related issues. I
have attempted to describe the affirmative and critical perspectives as
neutrally as possible, but both are probably exaggerated slightly here in
order to highlight differences between them.

The affirmative position holds that modernization (as exemplified by
the historical development of Western Europe and North America over
the last few centuries) has been basically successful. According to this
view, people in modern Western societies are happier, healthier and more
productive than any previous groups in human history. They enjoy great
freedom of expression as well as geographic and social mobility. Their
high material standard of living, the direct fruit of the dynamism of
capitalism and democracy, has permitted an unprecedented flowering
of culture and science. The affirmative view thus holds that the already
industrialized societies have the responsibility to help less developed
nations on the path to modernization. The advanced societies must also

forge ahead to solve the remaining mysteries of science and develop new technologies to make life even more pleasant. The affirmative perspective tends to focus on science, technology and industry as the driving forces of modernization and assumes that negative social and environmental consequences of scientific and technological development will be eventually solved as a result of the same dynamic process of growth. Democratic governments play an important, but not essential, role in fostering modernization.

In near total contrast, the critical perspective argues that modernization is nothing but a euphemistic term for the establishment of capitalist forms of industrialization and the oppressive social institutions that support them. Capitalist economic development is fostered by the control of wealth by a few and sustained by public schooling, police protection of property, reserve labour pools of unemployed urban poor, restrictions on democratic processes and mass media that reinforce free market and consumerist ideology. The critical perspective allows that certain levels of industrialization are indeed necessary and that the early phases of modernization had beneficial effects for the rising bourgeoisie, that is, the higher strata of society that had been dominated for centuries by the fusion of royal and clerical power. Whether through revolution or reform, new sectors of society such as the wealthier commercial classes gained access to political power and even greater economic resources. Enlightenment philosophers such as Locke, Smith and Kant provided justifications for this new order. Certain gains were made in the name of the poor masses, but the promise of a liberal society with equal opportunities for all went unfulfilled. In fact, the individuals produced by the social processes of capitalist industrialization are alienated and exploited in ways that for the most part perpetuate the previous outright domination of slaves by their masters or serfs by the nobility. Cultures have been fragmented, families torn apart, entire peoples dispersed, if not slaughtered – all for unnecessary increments in the standard of living of the well-to-do. This damage spread to the entire world in the nineteenth century as European colonialism took root in what is now known as the Third World. Wherever it gains a foothold, modernization sows alcoholism, drug addiction, ecological destruction, cultural chaos, crime and neurosis. The critical perspective thus argues that industrialized societies should seek to foster more harmonious relations with nature and among their own citizens. It also asserts that developing societies would do best not to emulate capitalist modernization. Instead, they should seek a path designed to meet basic human needs first. The critical perspective thus chooses to focus on the environmental, social, cultural and psychological consequences of modernization and tends to discount the achievements of scientific and technological development.

The affirmative and critical perspectives obviously focus on different aspects of the process of modernization as they develop their arguments and thus come to different conclusions. Their selective attention is not unmotivated. The affirmative perspective embodies at least an implicit political agenda: the expansion of the institutions of capitalism. My portrayal of the position above equates roughly with conservative political stances in Western Europe and the United States. The critical outlook tends to be more explicitly political since its advocates hope to disrupt the advance of capitalism and to stimulate social change towards fulfilment of the technological and social potential of industrialization. My description of the critical perspective comprehends a variety of positions on the left and probably coincides most closely with a democratic socialist outlook, but it also encompasses many elements of green politics.

In these contrasting perspectives, we glimpse the manner in which ideological positions operate in evaluations of the impact of modernization. The affirmative view tends to focus on material gains and creature comforts and contrasts political gains to previous eras. The critical view emphasizes the assessment of remaining material inequalities and human suffering in light of ideals which have not been achieved. The issue might be seen as matter of 'how far we have come' versus 'how far we have to go'.

Clearly one's stand on the issue is going to depend to some extent on one's position in society. The 'haves' and those that identify with them (the affirmative folks) tend to say that we have come a long way; the 'have nots' and their allies (the critical camp) stress either how far we have yet to go or that we have been going in the wrong direction. There is a third position on this issue, the liberal view, which is adopted by a group that strives to remain moderate and/or balanced in its political judgements. In general, the liberal position recognizes some of the social costs of capitalist development and tries to address them without calling into question the basic political and economic structures associated with capitalism. Much of this book could be seen as an articulation of my reasons for favouring a critical perspective over a liberal one. In this chapter I begin this exploration by laying out a sociological perspective on the emergence of modernity that provides an excellent foundation for understanding the societal origins of a wide variety of psychosocial pathologies.

SYSTEM AND LIFEWORLD

Jürgen Habermas (born 1929) is the leading spokesperson for the sociological perspective known as *critical theory*. This perspective received its primary impetus from the work of the Institute of Social Research, founded in Frankfurt, Germany, in 1923. The Institute counted among its collaborators at various points a number of well-known philosophers and social theorists: Max Horkheimer, Theodor Adorno, Herbert Marcuse and Erich Fromm, for example (cf. Jay 1973 and Held 1980 for very useful histories). Habermas worked with the Institute as a young man and now leads the second generation of what is known as the Frankfurt School of critical theory. His work already spans several decades and has evolved extensively, but it is possible to synthesize from his various texts a relatively consistent perspective on modernization. Helpful secondary accounts and critiques of Habermas's project are available in Held (1980), Schmid (1982), Thompson (1984), Bernstein (1985), Benhabib (1986), Ingram (1987), White (1988) and Arnason (1991). Here I present only the basic features of Habermas's perspective with an eye to drawing out their psychological implications. I begin by reviewing Habermas's views on the historical processes and social trends associated with moderniz-ation. The following sections, I must admit, are highly abstract, but I have attempted to provide concrete examples as often as possible.

Habermas first points out that societies consist of institutions and activi-ties that perform several essential functions. These can be divided roughly into the categories *system* and *lifeworld*. System refers to knowledge and activities related to the *material* reproduction of society: agricultural practices, childbirthing techniques, architectural and engineering methods, ways of transporting and exchanging goods, and so forth. Accompanying each of these practices is a set of information or knowledge that informs participants about what is the case in the objective world and how to do things. Physical survival of human communities depends on the effective practical application of various sorts of know-how.

Lifeworld refers to the socio-cultural basis for communication, social interaction, consensus formation and conflict resolution. As a sort of storehouse of collective cultural knowledge, the lifeworld makes possible the cultural, institutional and psychological reproduction of society. It creates spaces for the development, preservation, and *transformation* of ideas, decisions, beliefs, feelings, values and meanings. The lifeworld com-prises aspects of social life that have *symbolic* functions, rather than immediately practical aims: religious values, self-concepts, social norms, stories, ethical attitudes, artistic expressions and games.

Habermas asserts that prior to the modern era, system and lifeworld stood in quite a different relation to each other than they do now. This difference can be illustrated through an informal example that accents the impact of modernization on the lifeworld (as opposed to the develop-ments of the system which set up this effect). Imagine harvest time in any rural zone in 1700. The work was exceedingly tiresome. It was often carried out in horrendous conditions. The work of the harvest, however, was accompanied by a certain experience of community: work songs, communal cooking, stories told around bonfires at night, fistfights, dancing and music, disputes between workers and their bosses, funeral processions, games, feasts – an integrated set of practices and rituals that sustained both the material survival and the cultural identity of the community. We now can compare this slightly romanticized scene with a more contemporary one.

In the late twentieth century, many remnants of this past persist even in modernized rural zones. Perhaps a harvest parade or a harvest dance harks back to old times, or urban families seeking a change might camp out in the woods and sing songs around a fire. In general, however, agricultural production has been separated from community life and from home life. Now, in the most advanced agribusinesses, a few lone operators drive combine harvesters across vast scientifically-planned fields to skim the fruits of the earth. The produce is automatically processed for distribution in urban centres. What little remains of the premodern, integrated lifeworld in the rural zones is condensed into the farm operator's conversations with his wife in the evening or with the man who owns the silo or with a few friends at the diner.

I do not mean to imply that modern individuals live without access to the symbolic and cultural resources of a lifeworld, but that their everyday experience is less integrated with local and domestic systems of material production directly related to survival than they were in premodern days. Obviously, many cultural practices associated with rural living followed populations as they migrated to the cities and now coexist with urban living and industrial work. Nevertheless, a certain cleavage between system and lifeworld seems to have occurred.

Such changes in the relation between system and lifeworld can be understood as indirect effects of the rationalization of production associated with industrialization. As industrialization proceeds in any region of the world, a now familiar pattern of interwoven social displacements unfolds. The quest for efficiency in production and increased output leads to a separation of work activities from the home. Home-based craftsmanship and local labour-intensive agriculture are gradually replaced by mechanized production of food and goods controlled by larger enterprises. The efficiency of industrial production, in turn, gives rise to even greater concentration of both economic and political power in the cities. Farm workers displaced by mechanization of agricultural labour and rural youth drift towards the cities for work. Fuelled by new pools of labour, the city-based operations of both the market and the state expand and become increasingly bureaucratized in response to the growing complexity and velocity of industrial and commercial processes.

If one considers primarily economic and demographic effects, remarkable similarities exist between this process of modernization in the European and North American societies of the eighteenth and nineteenth centuries (cf. Thompson 1963; Wilensky and Lebeaux 1965; Brown 1976; Holton 1985) and that of Asian, African and Latin American regions in the twentieth century (cf. Alavi and Shanin 1982; Nash 1984; DuBois 1991). Since Third World modernization is directly affecting the lives of perhaps ten times as many people as did the European or North American processes, I have chosen to describe the process here in the present tense and not as something that has already transpired.

As industrialization proceeds to transform the material environment and the nature of the work day, people do what they can to participate in the familiar practices connected with the reproduction of their lifeworlds. They continue to sing songs to their babies, tell fairy tales, talk politics, celebrate marriages with kin, gossip, practise their religions. In these and a multitude of other ways, they sustain a realm of symbolic and communicative practices that help them define personal identities and social responsibilities, maintain hope and make sense of life in a more or less collective manner.

As modernization proceeds, Habermas argues, the relative contribution of the lifeworld to the direction of societal development declines. In a sense, the lifeworld shrinks as it becomes dissociated from the operations of the system. The internal logic of the system (to be specified further on) allows it to expand and evolve quite independently from lifeworld concerns. In other words, people's deeply felt ideas about what would constitute a good life become increasingly irrelevant to the choices made in order to foster industrial production and economic growth.

In light of this, Habermas (1970: 114) defines the 'threshold of modernity' in an intriguing manner. Modernity, he says, is established by the processes of rationalization that unfold when the requirements of the system gain superiority over the values embedded in the lifeworld. In this context, rationalization refers to the systematic co-ordination of human action so as to maximize the attainment of a goal. Rationalization occurs when traditional worldviews or practices are criticized, displaced and revised in light of values associated with scientific and technological development – values such as efficiency, productivity, objectivity, neutrality. The impact of rationalization on lifeworlds is dramatically illustrated when a residential community is destroyed in order to build a new factory or when the homelands of indigenous peoples are flooded by waters backed up by a hydroelectric dam (Ekins 1992). In more subtle ways, it occurs when, in the name of convenience or increased profit, stores stay open on the traditional day of rest, when a government sets up an office for handling disputes between citizens, and even when a family purchases a second television in order to satisfy the competing viewing interests of parents and children.

Habermas (1987) describes this initial phase of modernization as a progressive *uncoupling of system and lifeworld*. As the two realms separate, both become increasingly differentiated and 'rationalized' internally as well. In the system, production processes are constantly reviewed to improve efficiency and cut costs. Aspects of the lifeworld itself come to be evaluated according to new criteria. Rationalization entails not only new social practices, but is itself established by the imposition of new forms of reasoning and different bases for making and justifying claims about the world. Previously unquestioned sources of authority (elders, kings, priests) begin to have to justify their decisions and proclamations in terms of reasons.

Habermas shows that the social impact of this differentiation that accompanies modernization can be analysed in relation to several inherent facets of the lifeworld. As system and lifeworld are uncoupled, the latter breaks into three interrelated *structural components* that were previously more tightly interwoven at the experiential level: culture (knowledge and meaning systems), society (norms for ordered social interaction) and personality (identity).

Each structural component of the lifeworld has its own form of self-reproduction but is also sustained by the reproductive processes of the other two components. In the sphere of culture, *cultural reproduction* allows the interpretive work and knowledge of previous generations to be passed on. In the reproduction of society, *social integration* transmits the norms and legitimate institutional orders that provide solidarity and a sense of community. At the level of individual persons, *socialization* establishes the foundations for ego identity (selfhood) as well as capacities for social interaction. Socialization comprises primarily childrearing practices and education.

Figure 3.1 shows schematically how the structural components of the lifeworld interact to reproduce culture, society and personality. The columns of Figure 3.1 represent the structural components of the lifeworld. The rows refer to the processes that reproduce the lifeworld. Each box tells what is accomplished in a particular component of the lifeworld if reproduction processes are successful. The boxes along the diagonal represent the primary aims of reproduction processes. The off-diagonal boxes indicate how each structural component sustains reproduction processes in the two other spheres.

Habermas explains that, as the structures of the lifeworld are differentiated and rationalized, the genie of modernization escapes from the bottle. Culture and society separate from personality. Personality and society separate from culture, and society uncouples from culture and personality. These differentiations set up important new degrees of freedom that can be actualized through further differentiation and critical revision. For example, as the spheres of culture and society separate, social institutions are no longer governed directly by religious worldviews or other cosmovisions. With the differentiation of both culture and society from personality, individuals are freed to adopt customs selectively and to question tradition and social institutions as well as their own identities

Structural components / Reproductive processes	Culture	Society	Personality
Cultural reproduction	Transmission, critique, acquisition of cultural knowledge	Renewal of knowledge effective for legitimation	Reproduction of knowledge relevant to childrearing, education
Social integration	Immunization of a central stock of value orientations	Co-ordination of actions via intersubjectively recognized validity claims	Reproduction of patterns of social membership
Socialization	Enculturation	Internalization of values	Formation of identity

Figure 3.1 Reproductive processes associated with the structural components of the lifeworld

Source: Habermas 1987: 144

and social behaviour. In general, accepted ways of doing things culturally, socially and personally are opened to criticism and revision because their premodern coherence is disrupted by new forms of reasoning and the practices associated with them. Why this is so will require a more detailed discussion of the notion of rationality itself to which I turn in a moment.

The importance of the scheme laid out thus far is that it allows us to see how certain aspects of modernization could induce social pathology, including psychopathology. Habermas argues that any development that interferes with lifeworld processes related to the reproduction of society, culture or personality could disrupt one or more of the sources of meaning, social solidarity, or identity. These disruptions are experienced as *crises*. Figure 3.2 indicates the sorts of crises that can occur when the processes of cultural reproduction, social integration and socialization are disrupted. The boxes on the diagonal represent the direct effects of

Structural components / Distur-bances in the domain of	Culture	Society	Personality
Cultural reproduction	Loss of meaning	Withdrawal of legitimation	Crisis in orientation and education
Social integration	Unsettling of collective identity	Anomie	Alienation
Socialization	Rupture of tradition	Withdrawal of motivation	Psychopath-ologies

Figure 3.2 Crises in the lifeworld caused by disrupted reproductive processes
Source: Habermas 1987: 143

disruptions of reproduction processes in a given structural component. The off-diagonal boxes show indirect effects. For example, a sense of alienation invades the personality component of the lifeworld when reproductive processes of social integration break down. In other words, people feel estranged from social institutions when something goes wrong in the reproduction of social roles (since they constitute links between persons and society). As a result, they would experience crises in the establishment of personal identity.

As I pointed out earlier, the uncoupling of system from lifeworld sets up the potential for the various components of the lifeworld to be subjected to system imperatives, that is, to be reorganized in line with the requirements of the production system and related institutions. This can be observed in the various consequences of modernization. Cumbersome extended families break down in order to provide efficient, mobile child-

bearing units for urban, industrial labour. Heterogeneous cultural reproduction is streamlined through state-regulated mass education to include
only the essentials: literacy, numeracy and a sense of citizenship. Market
mechanisms such as advertising are developed to shape culture itself and
to produce a population interested in working primarily in order to
consume the products offered by the system. One could point to many
other ways that the system begins to encroach on lifeworld processes.
The effects of modernization seem to spread into every nook and cranny
of society.

The concepts of system and lifeworld give us a new perspective on
what is going on, but it may seem that Habermas has merely coined new
terms for industrialization (system) and tradition (lifeworld). How, then,
is Habermas not committing the errors signalled by Blumer (Chapter 2)
in attributing all sorts of social pathology to the development of the
industrial system? Habermas's answer would be that it is not industrialization *per se* that produces undesired social effects. Following Weber and
Marx, Habermas traces social pathology to the predominance of a limited
vision of rationality, one that originates in the human interest in exerting
technical control over the objective world. The application of this vision
of rationality has tended to decrease the value of other modes of reasoning and understanding involved in cultural reproduction and meaning-
construction. Habermas's account provides a concise framework within
which the question of modernity's impact on the psyche may be re-
examined. What still needs to be understood more clearly is what exactly
it is about modernization that disrupts the reproduction of the lifeworld.
To get at this, I sketch Habermas's views on the various modes of rationality, after which I examine in more detail his innovative claim that
psychopathology is generated not so much by modernization processes
themselves but by the form of rationality that guides them.

FORMS OF RATIONALITY

In the first volume of *The Theory of Communicative Action* (1984),
Habermas reconstructs the process by which the religious metaphysical
worldview of medieval Europe was gradually replaced by 'modern structures of consciousness'. One purpose of this reconstruction is to propose
a theory of modernity that 'explains the type of social pathologies that
are becoming increasingly visible' (Habermas 1984: x1). He approaches
this immense and problematic task through a reappropriation, in light of
his own theory of communicative action, of the main currents of sociological thought, including Marx, Weber, Durkheim, Mead and Parsons.

As I mentioned earlier, Habermas's entire argument depends on a
provocative formulation regarding the nature of rationality. The term
rationality is understood colloquially as pertaining to logical thinking in

conjunction with possession of knowledge. In Habermas's expanded notion, rationality refers to a wide variety of practices through which persons learn, speak and act in relation to different aspects of their world.

The fact that our everyday understanding of rationality is limited to the possession of facts and thinking in relation to them is itself a symptom of our embeddedness in the modern era. In the modern view, 'rational' persons use knowledge as an instrument for achieving their ends in a physical and social environment. It is assumed that if they have a correct definition of their environment (the 'truth'), they are more likely to be successful or effective in achieving their aims. They will select an appropriate instrument or means to accomplish a desired end. Habermas juxtaposes this form of *cognitive-instrumental rationality* to *communicative rationality*. The latter refers to experiences of coming to an understanding or consensus through a social, 'intersubjective' process of communication, argumentation and debate. In such processes, 'reasons' not necessarily linked to objective facts are generally considered valid to the extent that they are grounded in established social norms (*moral-practical* reasons) or in the private world of subjective experience (*aesthetic-expressive* reasons). In other words, persons can be said to be acting rationally if they can justify their actions through reference to the legitimate behavioural expectations of the common social world (norms) or to behaviour consistent with the consequences of a personal desire, mood or commitment. All these forms of rationality have in common the requirement that, potentially at least, persons in disagreement or conflict could come to a consensus through argumentation, that is, on the basis of reasons. Therefore, 'there is, on the side of persons who behave rationally, a willingness to expose themselves to criticism and, if necessary, to participate properly in argumentation' (Habermas 1984: 18).

Habermas points out that three modes of orientation to the world are implicit in his model of communicative rationality. These divide the world into three subworlds that moderns have no trouble distinguishing cognitively. These worlds are: the *objective* world of things, the *social* world of interpersonal relations, and the *subjective* world. Modern modes of orientation to the objective, social and subjective worlds stand in contrast to the *mythical* understanding of the world in which the three worlds are relatively undifferentiated.

PREMODERN VERSUS MODERN WORLDVIEWS

Habermas generalizes loosely from anthropological studies to construct an ideal type of the 'mythical' or premodern form of world orientation. The mythical orientation does not allow a clear distinction between nature and culture, between things and persons, between causes and motives, or between words and objects. Nature and society interpenetrate. Aspects of the world are interconnected in a vast web of similarities and differ-ences. There is nothing behind this surface to 'interpret'. Perceptual pro-cesses, operating concretely, construct an order in which nature is anthropomorphized and culture is naturalized. Where these concrete pro-cesses of understanding fail, and where human control of outcomes is impossible, magic is invoked, 'logically', as an explanation or in an attempt at gaining control. If this seems an unlikely state for the human mind to enter into, it may be helpful to recall that modern neuroses are accompanied by such magical attitudes towards major segments of the neurotic's world. Neurotics act as if the world really is the way they imagine it to be and at some level they expect to gain control over their situations by thus deceiving themselves.

Given this portrayal of the mythical worldview, we need to know how it is transformed into the modern worldview. Habermas's model focuses not on the historical aspects of demythologization, but on its structural consequences in terms of the differentiation of the three worlds listed above. Basically, demythologization involves a desocialization of nature and a denaturalization of society. Nature comes to be experienced less as a whole of which one is a part and more as an object to be subjected to human control through the technical implementation of scientific knowl-edge. Society also comes to be taken not as a natural order, but instead as a system whose norms and laws can be engineered for maximum efficiency and stability. In a complementary process, language and the world to which language refers are differentiated from each other. Hopes for magical control of the environment through incantation, for example, necessarily collapse in this process of differentiation.

As this objectivated world of things and the norm-regulated social world become differentiated, a separate 'inner', subjective world arises. Subjective life is enhanced because only against the background of the objective and the social world can one's hopes and ideas prove baseless or one's plans prove unacceptable. Individuation – the production of the person as an individual endowed with a subjective reality – thus begins with the collapse of the mythical totality.

In sum, Habermas asserts, against the claims of certain anthropologists, that we cannot define the mythical understanding of the world as a rational one. It fails to meet the requirements of communicative ration-ality, because in contrast to the ideal type of the modern worldview:

> Mythical worldviews are not understood by members as interpretive systems that are attached to cultural traditions, constituted by internal relations of meaning, symbolically related to reality, and connected with validity claims – and thus exposed to criticism and open to revision.
>
> (Habermas 1984: 52–53)

Drawing upon the theory of cognitive development proposed by Jean

Piaget, Habermas likens the rise of modern structures of consciousness to the 'decentration of an egocentric understanding of the world' (Habermas 1984: 69) through learning processes that successively devalue certain kinds of reasons. Statements about the world take on the status of *interpretations* that can be subjected to criticism and revision. Even in the modern world, essential interpretations (and the interpretive work of previous generations) are passed on through socialization practices and education. These convictions form the basis for the lifeworld, which can now be construed as a background structure of activities, understandings and expectations against which subjectivity plays in complex *symbolic* processes.

This complexity is due, first of all, to the fact that the lifeworld's survival depends on interconnected processes of cultural activity, social integration and the socialization of new personal identities. The achievement of personal identity depends on community solidarity and embeddedness in a cultural tradition. The reverse also seems to be the case; 'living' traditions and communities depend for their survival on their ability to foster new personal identities that keep individuals sufficiently committed to them. The matter becomes even more complex when one notes that each of these interactions between structural components of the lifeworld relies on forms of symbolic communication. It is as if new members of society must learn to speak multiple languages in order to interpret what is going on around them in different spheres of society.

We touched earlier on the exciting hypothesis that follows from Habermas's line of reasoning. If the reproduction and 'health' of human society depends on successful transmission of the lifeworld to successive generations we can suppose that interference with the *symbolic* aspects of these processes would produce the sorts of symptoms of which moderns usually complain: meaninglessness, destabilization of collective identities, confusion, lack of direction, decreased legitimacy of authorities, alienation and psychopathologies – in short, all the forms of social pathology listed in Figure 3.2. Habermas indeed argues that the nature of capitalist modernization has been such that symbolic communicative activities have been increasingly disrupted and displaced by cognitive-instrumental forms of rationality that characterize the natural and physical sciences as well as their technological and administrative applications.

Grounding his thesis in Weber's notions regarding the impact of Western rationalism, which can be equated in large part with cognitive-instrumental rationality, Habermas shows how each sphere of the lifeworld – society, culture and personality – is affected by the process of modernization. In the sphere of society, Western rationalism contributed to the differentiation and development of the *capitalist market economy* and the *modern bureaucratic state*. The internal organization and interaction of these segments of society are governed by *formal law*. In the sphere of culture, Western rationalism provoked a series of rationalizations that progressively undermined religious worldviews and the ethically meaningful nature of the universe. Each time empirical knowledge advanced, or the capacity for technical control and efficiency increased through better organization, the truth claims of theological-cosmological worldviews were challenged further. Power shifted into the hands of those who achieved goals through the application of cognitive-instrumental rationality. As this happened, the sphere of morality and law also broke free from direct religious control and legal norms became subject to debate or manipulation by other agencies.

As the process of modernization continues, the different modes of rationality tend to become isolated in separate 'orders of life'. The resulting divisions present a serious problem to individuals who need to form personal identities capable of integrating the several modes of rationality. Habermas writes:

> Cognitive-instrumental, moral-practical, and aesthetic expressive orientations of action ought not to become so independently embodied in antagonistic orders of life that they overcome the personality system's average capacity for integration and lead to permanent conflicts between lifestyles.
>
> (Habermas 1984: 245)

Such lifestyle conflicts are experienced in countless ways in modern society: for example, by scientifically-trained professionals who were raised in traditional religions, by persons with strong artistic inclinations forced to do routinized work, by youth who enter the military, and so on. But Habermas's point is that most modern individuals are likely to experience the external conflicts between orders of life and the social crises generated by them as conflict at the level of personal identity.

THE MODERN PERSONALITY

Still following Weber, Habermas lays more groundwork for understanding the impact of modernization on personality structures. Associated with the foregoing developments in culture and society, Weber posited a change in the motivational bases of individual conduct. According to Weber's thesis, this change affected not only social behaviour but also the organization of personality in such a way that a 'methodical conduct of life' became widespread among the social classes associated with the rise of capitalism in Europe. Weber argued that the replacement of Catholicism by the 'Protestant ethic' encouraged a cognitive-instrumental attitude not only in dealing with the natural environment but also towards inner experience and interpersonal relations (Mommsen 1987). This 'objectivating' stance – one which renders as inert objects processes that are dynamically symbolic – allowed for increased self-control through a denial of 'disruptive' aesthetic-expressive urges. Protestant requirements for self-control transcended those of Catholic asceticism with its devices of celibacy, poverty and the cloister. The Calvinists and Puritans insisted on the elimination of erotic desire and pleasure in the midst of family living, the curtailment of unnecessary consumption regardless of wealth, and the maintenance of rationality despite embeddedness in the sensuality of the world. The accumulation of capital and its wise investment can be seen as a correlate of these attitudes.

Habermas focuses on the types of rationality fostered by Protestant ethical rationalism, but I will permit myself to insert a few ideas about what might have been occurring at the level of personality structures as a way of fleshing out the relevance of Habermas's perspective to this inquiry. One could suppose, for example, that personality structures within Western societies have differed from generation to generation over the last few hundred years or so primarily in the relations between the agencies of the psychical structure described by Freud, that is, between the id, ego and superego. (Here I use a psychoanalytic framework because it will be familiar to most readers. No judgement as to its general validity is being made at this point.) These intrapsychic relations would vary according to the class positions and religious cultures of the subjects involved, but, in line with Habermas, one could suppose that the rise of the bourgeois individual in liberal society was accompanied by increasing elaboration and complexity of both cognitive (ego) and moral-ethical (superego) structures. These new psychological organizations were supported by complementary societal and interpersonal processes in the civil order, the press, governing bodies and families. The goal of socialization (childrearing and education) became autonomous individuation – the production of subjects who were more capable than previous generations of sustained reflection on and revision of life plans and projects in the light of both instrumental aims and communicative (ethical, aesthetic and expressive) rationalities. Such were the signs of differentiation and rationalization of the personality component of the lifeworld.

As new systems for the technological control of nature and social administration spread and became routinized in the nineteenth century, the historical juncture we know as the Enlightenment passed. In a reduced social sphere and for a brief time, the ethics of the Enlightenment world-view may have sustained an admirable balance between system and lifeworld. The bourgeois individual (particularly the father) played an important role in sustaining this balance through his actions as public citizen, productive agent and head of household. But this balance could not be sustained, mostly because of the combined effects of the capitalist economy and the bureaucratic nation-state, as well as the fact that both relied on the domination of women, children, the working class and distant colonies. As Marx was quick to point out, in practice, the Enlightenment ideal was mostly ideology.

Subsequently, the citizens of the new modernity were increasingly subjected to what Habermas calls the *colonization of the lifeworld*. This refers to the extension of cognitive-instrumental rationalities into more and more spheres of the lifeworld through the operation of social steering mechanisms necessary for efficient social administration and successful market operations: public schools, legal systems, market surveys, labour laws, various forms of surveillance and testing, prisons and mental asylums, social work, personnel departments and advertising. These institutional developments became necessary in order to maintain stability and offset the basic contradiction of capitalist economic development. This contradiction is neatly described by Ingram:

> The accumulation of capital is pitted against the conditions necessary for its production, consumer demand. Unlimited development of labor-saving, cost-efficient technologies leads to overproduction; accumulation of capital by fewer and fewer investors goes hand in hand with the progressive impoverishment of unemployed consumers. Without able consumers willing to dispose of the surfeit of capital, the accumulation process cannot but reverse itself, the subsequent depression revealing the inherent injustice of the market and its pretension to be an impartial system of exchange.
>
> (Ingram 1987: 123)

This systemic crisis in the economic sphere masks fundamental inequalities stemming from class divisions within society. When the system falters, class antagonisms are fuelled and new attempts to restore social order are required (see Baran and Sweezy 1966.) Here we see one of the major forces behind the ongoing infiltration of the lifeworld by systemic operations.

Developing a recurrent theme in the work of the Frankfurt School, Habermas claims that the colonization of the lifeworld means that individuals are less inclined to orient themselves by values such as those embedded in the ego ideals or superego processes. Their decisions about courses of action are instead subjected directly to the imperatives of the administered environment. In the resulting scenario, the state and the market project the existing or near future reality as the ideal, filling the space in which alternative collective and personal ideals could be formulated through ongoing interaction and debate. The individual's task becomes one of adjustment or 'fitting in' rather than individuation or self-realization through intersubjective communication. Advanced capitalist modernization thus triggers a decline of the autonomous ego. Modern subjects objectively have more choices, more concrete options, but the frames within which they choose are themselves manufactured to a large

extent to coincide with market and state imperatives for social reproduction. This structuring of choice is not comparable to the cultural,
aesthetic and ethical mediation of life options and commitments by the
communication processes of a flourishing lifeworld. Where one style of
choice is mechanical or automatic, a result of operant conditioning, the
other is characterized by the meaningfulness that stems from dialogue,
understanding and conscious choice (Narr 1985).

THE LOSS OF MEANING

We are now in a position to ask: Is the colonization of the lifeworld
related to the 'loss of meaning' that is said to characterize modern experience? Habermas's argument clearly demonstrates that modern individuals
could be seen as increasingly cut off from the communicative experiences
in the lifeworld that provide the basis for the construction of meaning.
They are thrown back on their increasingly isolated selves to establish
some sort of unity and coherence in their identities as well as in their
life plans. Since this private realm has been largely stripped of the contexts
of cultural and material reproduction in which meanings were once available through complex symbolic processes of communication, the individual comes up empty-handed – or with a handful of prefabricated
dreams. In the private search for images of gratifying forms of life, the
predominant ones are those supplied not by the impoverished lifeworld
but by the system. Thus begins the desperate rat race to earn enough
money to purchase system-designed lifestyle packages to organize one's
leisure time.

As the painful consequences of the colonization of the lifeworld become
obvious, it is easy to lose track of the positive side of the developments
associated with modernization. The diminution of the collective lifeworld
has potentially beneficial psychological consequences as well. Following
a powerful, extended Habermasian argument by Luke and White, we can
note that the differentiation of system from lifeworld 'gives actors the
conceptual means for constructing a self-critical perspective', 'provides
the possibility of entertaining and evaluating alternative interpretations'
in the natural, social and subjective worlds and 'allows agents a degree
of reflexive penetration of the hitherto impenetrable horizon of their
"lifeworld" '. New critical capacities are then 'integrated into the ongoing
reproduction of his lifeworld'. Living becomes a matter of using 'interpretive and evaluative skills' to arrive at an intersubjective understanding of
problems rather than knee-jerk adherence to 'normative prescriptions
grounded in opaque sources of authority' (Luke and White 1985: 26–29).

Habermas helps us grasp another dimension of the impact of modernity
in his work on moral development, in which he draws heavily on
Kohlberg's model of preconventional, conventional and postconventional

stages. The transition from the traditional, norm-guided behaviour of the conventional stage to the postconventional stage in which all norms and practices can be subjected to criticism parallels the impact of moderniz-ation on traditional lifeworlds. When, due to the objective, decentred gaze of the modern person, traditions are seen as mere traditions, they lose their naturalness in the same way that adolescents begin to see the unnaturalness of the particular social norms to which they are asked to submit. Habermas points out that if one imagines

> a critical instant in which the individual for the first time – yet pervas-ively and intransigently – assumes a hypothetical attitude toward the normative context of his lifeworld, we can see the nature of the prob-lem every person must deal with in passing from the conventional to the postconventional level of moral judgment. The social world of legitimately regulated interpersonal relations, a world to which one was naïvely habituated and which was unproblematically accepted, is abruptly deprived of its quasi-natural validity.
>
> (Habermas 1990: 126)

Just as the adolescent must struggle to reconstruct a stable moral orientation to the world, modern individuals struggle to erect a new social order in a world where norms have been problematized because all norms can be called into question and need justification if they are to serve as the basis for consensual action. The democratic ideal of modernity pro-vided the plan for how we should proceed collectively to re-establish a rational order in the post-traditional chaos. We were to achieve this through rational discourse and the equal participation in consensus forma-tion of all those affected by social decisions. For this democratic ideal to be realized, however, it needed to be incorporated into a wide range of social institutions. But the institutions associated with capitalist moderniz-ation, because of their emphasis on competition, status and efficiency, have resisted the extension of the democratic ideal into the sphere of work and have made only partial use of postconventional, post-traditional structures of moral judgement and related non-competitive motivations that modernity makes possible. Instead, capitalist institutions have primar-ily fostered instrumental attitudes towards the natural, social and subjec-tive worlds, downgrading moral concerns and aesthetics to the sphere of the irrational. Thus, in the absence of strong movements towards partici-patory democracy, as yet unaffected zones of the lifeworld are increasingly dominated by subsystems determined by the operations of money and political power.

As Luke and White point out, a primary aim of liberal society was to respect the separateness of the public and private realms. But in modern capitalist societies, the two spheres merge as the needs of the state and the corporation are directly internalized by individuals in their identities and value systems:

> Such identity linkages, in turn, allow professional experts in the state and the firm to regulate individuals more closely inasmuch as they define the needs extended to individuals as reified scripts of normal behaviour through the media, mass education, or professional expertise and through packages of material goods provided by corporate manufacture and commerce.
>
> (Luke and White 1985: 37)

In this system, consumption is a way of investing in new productive forces rather than just a reward for production.

The distinction between private and public realms was blurred further as

> private sector firms ... teamed up with the blessing of public-sector state agencies to regulate the consumption of goods and services of private individuals in the privacy of their homes as part of the larger public interest of constant economic growth.
>
> (Luke 1989: 98)

In North America and Western Europe, this fusion of public and private spheres coincides roughly with the transition from entrepreneurial to corporate capitalism in the mid-twentieth century.

To summarize, the colonization of the lifeworld is a mechanism by which advanced capitalist society stabilizes itself. Its crises in the economic sphere are deflected into the lifeworld realms of culture, society and personality. Among the prices paid for this stability are the loss of meaning, the destruction of solidarity and psychological crisis. '[W]hen steering crises – that is, perceived disturbances of material production – are successfully intercepted by having recourse to lifeworld resources, pathology arises in the lifeworld' (Habermas 1987: 385).

Habermas particularly notes how the identity problems of contemporary adolescents and young adults reflect these system/lifeworld relations. Experiences at home and school have little to do with the adoption of adult roles. As Habermas puts it:

> When the conditions of socialization in the family are no longer functionally in tune with the organizational membership conditions that the growing child will one day have to meet, the problems that young people have to solve in their adolescence become insoluble for more and more of them.
>
> (Habermas 1987: 388)

Much of Habermas's recent work (1984, 1987) examines the conditions under which the colonization of the lifeworld might be reversed. In particular, he focuses on the forms of communication that are essential if citizens are to participate equally in the resolution of social conflict and the formation of consensus about possible futures. He refers to such capacities to express one's needs and participate with others in decisions about collective life as *communicative competence*. In Habermas's earlier work (1971), he frequently refers to the psychological obstacles to undistorted communication and, in his later work, he continues to suggest that the psychological dimension of these issues must be addressed (1987: 389).

The sociological framework elaborated here on the basis of Habermas's work suggests that it will be profitable to focus our inquiry on these questions: How exactly should we understand the impact of capitalist modernization on the development of personality? What aspects of the colonization of the lifeworld interfere with symbolic processes and communicative competence? What sorts of psychopathology can be traced to this interference?

In the next chapter I present an overview of the early development or formation of the psyche in order to begin addressing these questions from a perspective that is simultaneously socio-cultural and psychological.

Chapter 4

The formation of the psyche

The proliferation of personality theories during the twentieth century is itself an effect of modernity. The interest in broad perspectives on the nature of the individual such as those developed by Freud, Jung, Maslow, Fromm, Rogers and Horney stems in part from the displacement of theological visions of selfhood by secularization. Modern theories of personality can be seen as answering questions about the purpose of life and the goals of human development. Interest in theories of personality is also due to concerns about individuality fostered by the anonymity of life in mass society. Finally, concerns about personality are linked to the concerns of administrative steering systems which have found it necessary or profitable to develop more refined bureaucratic responses to manage individual differences such as 'deviance', 'giftedness' and 'mental illness'.

Obviously, we cannot step outside history and select a view of personality that is not in some way a product of modernity. In fact, my strategy will be the opposite. I will simply acknowledge this interpenetration of social and intellectual processes and select aspects of contemporary theory that are most relevant to understanding the formation of the psyche in the modern scene.

Up to this point, my analysis of the psychological impact of modernity has been hindered because I could not be sure that readers share a basic set of concepts referring to the psyche and its development. I have occasionally used basic Freudian terms, assuming that these were generally understood. I have also used the more colloquial terms employed in social psychology – attitudes, values, emotions. But in order to build on the perspective developed by Habermas, we will need a common terminology to refer to various aspects of subjective experience. This will not be a simple matter, for there must be as many competing theories of personality and psychological development as there are notions of modernization. In fact, every formal or informal student of psychology has his or her own favourite theory with an attendant set of criteria for determining what makes the theory a good one.

Rather than argue about which theory might be the best, I will adopt the view that all theories of personality are essentially elaborate metaphors or conceptual frameworks laid over the vibrant reality of real persons and their varied subjectivities. They are attempts to translate realms of personal experience and behaviour into language and to recognize some sort of order in these realms. Theories vary in respect to the particular zones of experience they choose to articulate. The specific realms chosen for conceptual elaboration by theorists themselves depend on numerous ideological, personal and practical factors. Therefore, the problem of choosing one theory over another is not as crucial as it may seem, for the core elements of one theory can, to a large extent, be translated into the terms of another.

For most of this chapter I set aside concerns about particular social contexts that may impinge on individual development and focus on the subjective pole of experience around which the psyche develops in the early stages of socialization.

THE STRUCTURING OF THE PSYCHE

It is unusual to hear the term 'psyche' these days. In psychological discussions, instead of psyche one usually hears 'personality' or 'self'; in philosophy, 'mind', 'consciousness' or 'subjectivity'; and in theology, 'spirit' or 'soul'. I have chosen to use the term psyche here because, although it has a loose meaning in Freudian psychoanalysis and a more precise definition within the psychological theory of Jung, it is not used colloquially and suffers less from the confusion associated with the more prevalent terms listed above.

The word *psyche* comes directly from the ancient Greek, which meant literally 'breath', and gradually evolved into the figurative equivalent of our 'soul'. Interestingly, some authors have argued that the evolution of the term's use in ancient Greek paralleled the emergence of Western philosophical thought and a new concept of personhood as a being endowed with autonomous rationality (Snell 1960).

I will employ the term *psyche* to signify a person's relatively enduring global mode of relating self to world and world to self. The concept of the psyche includes conscious as well as nonconscious mental and emotional experience. It thus encompasses all aspects of the ongoing process that synthesizes ideas, affects, memories, perceptions, values, images, plans – in short, everything that we usually lump casually in the category of 'self'.

The general perspective that addresses most profoundly the formation of the psyche as a complex of emotion, memory, experience and meaning is known as *psychodynamic psychology*. Launched by the fierce dedication of scholars such as Freud and Jung, psychodynamic thinking quickly became a prominent worldview in the capitals of Europe in the early twentieth century. The Second World War brought many psychodynamic thinkers to North America, for example, Erich Fromm and Erik Erikson. The repercussions of this perspective are still felt pervasively in the realms of culture, politics, arts and science. Within psychiatry and clinical psychology, many variants of psychodynamic thought have developed, each of which has a particular stance in relation to the general field of psychoanalysis (Frosh 1987; Jacoby 1975).

The account I present here synthesizes numerous perspectives associated with the line of thinking that emerged during the twentieth century as Freud's psychoanalytic theory developed into *ego psychology* and, later, *object relations* theory. Specialists will note influences from the overlapping but frequently contradictory positions of Klein, Kernberg and Lacan. This view of psychological development leaves out many elements that some readers would label as essential, including, for example, the Oedipus complex, aspects of cognitive development, forms of social learning such as imitation and modelling, development in later childhood and adolescence, and so forth. My purpose in excluding many of these important topics is to provide a basic scheme to set up later discussions of how individuals internalize their experiences with others in conjunction with emotional development. Proponents of any subschool of psychodynamic psychology as well as any other major approach to early personality development will find that many key themes are totally overlooked here. Furthermore, almost every basic point that has been made about early psychological development has been challenged in recent years with the rapid growth of *critical* developmental psychology (cf. Broughton 1987). I thus must ask the specialist to accept for the moment this general framework as a vantage point from which to consider the most basic claims that might be made about the impact of social arrangements on the psyche. (Similar summaries of psychological development, from slightly different theoretical perspectives, can be found in Allingham 1987; Greenspan 1989; and Bacal and Newman 1990.)

The basic task here is to describe the development of the psyche in such a way as to explain the formative role of significant others while simultaneously accounting for the gradual development of 'autonomous' subjective processes. In doing so, several questions are addressed: How do human infants develop to become active participants in family, culture, and society? How do they separate psychologically from their caretakers to become 'individuals'? How do they organize basic experiences of pleasure and pain into variegated emotional states and use these in developing social identities?

Why are these the key questions? Why focus on separation and individuation? Basically, these are domains that are relevant to the sphere of personality reproduction and identity development in Habermas's model of the lifeworld. These themes are also linked to most forms of psychopathology in that the latter can be comprehended as disturbances of self in relation to others.

We begin, not with the infant, but with the expecting parent(s). An interpersonal, psychological 'space' pre-exists a child's birth. Depending on social class, culture and individual circumstances of the parents, this space is characterized by a set of expectations, conditions and desires. Some infants, for example, will be received into a hungry, dependent space in which Baby has to make Mummy and Daddy happy. Others arrive in a sort of excluding space where there is actually little room for them in the subjective life of the caretakers; the infant's needs are met as just one of many chores. The specific style of parenting the child encounters is itself the product of a complex lifeworld process in which ideological trends and cultural practices become manifest via personal family preoccupations.

Whatever sort of space the infant encounters, its task is basically the same. It must learn what it can from interactions with the environment and its caretakers in order to survive physically and socially. It must simultaneously learn to sense where its own physical and psychological space begins and ends. The physical end of this process is complicated enough; fortunately, the basic apparatus for perception, sensation, and physical relatedness to the environment is a natural endowment. Meanwhile, the psychological challenge faced by the infant is so enormous that it could be argued that no human has yet been equal to it. This may seem pessimistic, but it does account for the sense one develops with age that even the best people one knows are in some way seriously flawed or limited. Such deficits are usually seen as the forgivable limitations of 'healthy' persons, but one could argue that even they would benefit from an expanded emotional repertoire and ideological self-criticism or reconstruction. We can see why this is so as we examine the early development of the psyche in greater detail.

According to many perspectives on psychological development, the infant's world consists of a rather chaotic collection of perceptions and sensations of interactions, body parts and physical objects. What is self and what is other is not clear to the infant. Long before a sense of what is inside and outside can develop, the infant begins to organize experience into categories of pleasure and pain, warm and cold, sharp and soft, and so forth, as guided by the five senses and feedback from internal organs.

These dichotomous distinctions become extremely important because they provide the bodily and emotional foundations for *enculturation* into symbol systems related to good and bad, and later, right and wrong. Freud gave us hints about such processes in essays such as 'Formulations on the two principles of mental functioning' (1911) and 'Negation' (1925). In these essays he asserted the primacy of the body's drive to maximize pleasure and minimize pain in the early structuring of the psyche. For example, Freud suggests that the bodily prototype of spitting out bad-tasting objects serves as a template for the primitive psychic defence called splitting. At an even more primary level, the nervous system's mechanisms for dealing with excess enervation prefigure later psychic strategies associated with repression and other defence mechanisms. Through such processes, the 'centre' of the experience of self is set up in contrast to feelings and impulses that would disrupt that centre.

Contemporary French psychoanalysis (see Elliott 1992) also emphasizes the importance of these prelinguistic, corporeal processes in establishing and maintaining the sense of self. In the collection of feeling states, memories and sensations that are avoided or rejected as not pleasant, we see the precursors of the psychic structure known as the *unconscious*. In some views, such as Lacan's, this is seen as an alienation from true subjectivity, an entry into a fictional or imaginary order (Boothby 1991). Others would see it as an accomplishment that fends off psychosis and allows further cognitive development.

Inherited temperamental factors, such as sensitivity, emotionality and activity level, obviously play a role in the manner in which pleasure and pain are differentiated, but the infant's interactions with caretakers are probably primary in determining the structuring of the psyche. This is so because early interactions between caretakers and the infant tend to be focused on exactly those experiences that are associated with pleasure and pain, such as feeding, play, the presence or absence of a parent, and so on. It is well known that even an active, healthy baby can become listless if it experiences little interaction and emotional warmth with its caretakers. Weak, sensitive babies begin to thrive under a regimen of attention and warm interaction. So, the character of a father's response to his baby's cry, the sort of expressive stimulation a mother gives while nursing, and any other interaction related to the infant's distress, excitement or pain is integrated into a primitive memory system that becomes the foundation of the psychic capacity for a sense of self and for meaningful experience (Kernberg 1977). This corporeal-emotional structure forms what one is tempted to call the 'core' of the psyche, were it not so misleading to spatialize a process that is not localizable but rather a dialectic of temporal experience and neurophysiological structure.

In the next phase of psychic development, the lifeworld of the infant becomes articulated along another dimension. Repeated interactions with caretakers and bodily experiences with physical objects begin to establish perceptual and cognitive differentiations between self and not-self. At first, this must be experienced as a vague emotional (non-linguistic) glimpse of the fact that 'Here I am', 'That hand is attached to me' or 'I moved that ball'. Given the added success the infant has in getting what it needs or wants if it pulls together sensations, perceptions and memory traces to co-ordinate its actions, it is not surprising that a primordial form of self-experience – a *body-ego* – becomes possible at this stage. Its boundaries are, of course, not well established. In the controversial view of Lacan (1966/1977), the establishment of an ego depends entirely on a sort of identification with a mirror image of self as perceived by others in order to accomplish this amalgamation of previously unorganized experiences. A very important consequence of this is that, even in adulthood, we can never actually clear others out of the space we experience as self. Self-experience is always experience of self-in-relation-to-other, or better yet, self-as-other. This may sound strange, but it is an insight that underlies much recent theorizing in the human sciences, especially approaches that emphasize the linguistic and symbolic aspects of selfhood (Elliott 1992).

Making this phase of psychic development even more complex is the fact that the budding self/other distinction proceeds in connection with the differentiation of pain and pleasure. The psyche follows the body's *telos*, serving to guide the infant away from pain and towards pleasure. This can be accounted for only to a certain extent by behaviourist concepts of reinforcement and punishment, because, from the earliest moments, social signs mediate development. Through various forms of *communication* with others, the child's attention is focused on the more pleasurable aspects of the psychic lifeworld and withdrawn from objects or impulses that are painful, overstimulating or otherwise to be 'negated'. Experiences of self thus emerge in connection with the child's selection of available pleasant or interesting modes of attending to the world. Since these modes do not operate in a vacuum, but are always at least implicitly social, a cornerstone of meaningfulness in experience lies here – in the socially mediated relation of one's own desires and intentions towards the world.

To summarize developments to this point: During the first year or two of life the infant needs to learn to manage experiences of pain and pleasure psychically and to begin to differentiate self from other. These accomplishments are possible thanks to the guiding and channelling provided by caretakers through their gestures, facial expressions, utterances and ways of handling the child's body, all of which are, in turn, linked to their perceptions of the child's needs, expressions and gestures. The basic structure of the psyche is thus established through a long series of communicative interactions between body (the infant) and culture (the caretakers' actions in relation to the child).

THE STYLING OF THE PSYCHE

The basic psychic structure we have described already contains elements of what we know as character, personality or even identity – the traits that distinguish us as individuals – but subsequent child development is crucial in determining personal *style*. In using the term style, I am referring to ideas developed by Shapiro (1965), Schafer (1976) and Stromberg (1992). These scholars argue that we must shift our focus away from the metaphor of psychic 'structure' since such thinking inevitably leads to questions about the location of substructures or the mechanisms by which they produce their effects, such as, Where is the unconscious? or, How does the superego repress an impulse? They prefer to focus on characteristics of action and communication that can be best described as stylistic. For example, it is more accurate to say simply that a person is acting seductively but speaking in a rejecting tone than to attribute this contradiction to desires that exist somewhere in a repressed unconscious or to a superego conflict. Such styles are often linked to what have been previously called defence mechanisms, which are basically ways of finding compromises between human desires and social expectations. As we begin to focus on style, it is important to remember that style is mediated by the structural dimensions we have already discussed. If those dimensions are forgotten, one tends to slide into an overly cognitive view that ignores the impact of dynamic unconscious processes.

Returning now to our discussion of the developing psyche, we may examine some of the processes that lead to different personality styles. First, it is important to note that the psychic differentiation of self from other is quite anxiety-provoking. In fact, just as the strong bonding and emotional attachment between an infant and its caretakers provides a sense of security later in life, an experience of anxiety may always be associated with vague memories of early separation experiences. Since anxiety impels a move towards fusion with the caretaker, the first conscious experiences of self as *psychologically* separate are likely to be those that occur in conjunction with interactions that have pleasant and warm tones, as in face-to-face play that makes a baby laugh and coo. Later, imitative mirroring games serve a similar function, supplying the infant with concrete images of its own emotional states and expressive style. All such experiences provide the foundation for the emotional capacity of basic trust (Erikson 1950), without which the successful resolution of subsequent development crises is unlikely. Again, we see that the ways in which caretakers interact with infants – that is, the specific culturally mediated practices brought to bear on the child – are primary determinants of the mode of subjective experience that the child will carry forward to address later developmental tasks.

This does not imply that an infant's experience must be manipulated to contain as few unpleasant experiences as possible. Experiences of pain, frustration and discomfort provide opportunities to develop defensive and coping strategies that are also essential to the process of self–other differentiation. It should be clear, however, that just as a child runs to a trusted parent when in pain or frightened, the newly differentiated self tends to slide back into states of self–other fusion when threatened. Such defensive regression indicates a lack of self–other differentiation. Regression kicks in as a way of dealing with prohibited impulses or conflicting feelings and desires. The particular personality style one adopts is ultimately related to the ways in which the experiences of self and other are fused or differentiated in relation to basic human impulses. These 'ways' are suggested by cultural training in early childhood, for example, by parental example or suggestions that angry feelings be either suppressed, displaced or expressed verbally.

Culture becomes important in other ways when the child begins to acquire language and to subject itself psychoemotionally to the moral order in which it will live its life. Depending on the culture, this phase of development may end as early as age 6 or 7 or may be prolonged through adolescence and early adulthood.

Beginning in early toddlerhood, the task of psychic development is to establish a secure 'centre' which will serve as the locus of the experience of 'I-ness' (Barratt 1984). One should not be misled, however, by the use of the terms 'centre' or 'I' into thinking that this is the centre of the psyche in any sense. This space is only a centre in the sense that it is where one senses that one psychically is. In this sense, it corresponds to the Freudian ego, the site at which conflicts are resolved and decisions are made. As I indicated above, cultural training and moral conditioning provide the pathways along which this experiencing of self in relation to others is channelled. How does this come about?

As a child experiences approval and disapproval from its caretakers, traces of these interactions are organized in relation to previously existing emotional meaning structures (pleasure/pain, self/other). This splitting process allows self-experience to coalesce around images (memories) of interactions that are positively toned or pleasurable: for example, emotionally toned representations of nice mummy, funny daddy and happy baby would foster the development of a differentiated self-image on baby's part as part of a triad. Similarly, negatively toned experiences tend to be cut off from self-experience (as in crying fits, fear reactions and physical pain), since they cannot be meaningfully integrated with the still fragile core of positive self-representations. It would produce severe anxiety, for example, if the happy baby self-image were to coincide with a daddy-about-to-lose-his-temper image. If these states could be put into words, they might be expressed as amalgamations of feelings like [bad/daddy(me)/hurt] or [mummy(me)/gone]. This retreat from selfhood can be seen in the way that it is difficult to reason with even older children when they are in such a state – they have to collect them*selves* first. Not only children have problems with differentiating self and other when images of self and other are connected to negative feeling states. Psychic differentiation of negative images of self and other remains difficult throughout life. In fact, the adult psyche may often regress to primitive states of self–other fusion as a defensive move when more advanced forms of anxiety management are not possible. In such states of fusion, images of self–and-other tend to be idealized, creating feelings of omnipotence and grandiosity.

The final consequential stage of psychic development establishes the capacity for *ambivalence* in regard to the emotional qualities associated with representations of self and others. This refers to the simultaneous existence of positively and negatively toned valences in an image of self or other. This is a particularly difficult task for the developing psyche for it means linking images that have been kept apart earlier to defend the fragile core of the self. Ambivalence is achieved, for example, when a caretaker begins to be perceived as capable of both kindness and hostility, or of both weakness and strength. In the process of building its own style of self-experience, the child's psyche necessarily clings to *idealized* images of caretakers, and banking on the strength of these, forms positive images of itself. So, as idealized images of others crumble in repeated confrontations with the realities of human interactions, the tenuous idealized self is also threatened with collapse and when it does, the experience of depression is at hand.

We now have the tools we need to understand the emotional foundations influenced by cultural training and moral conditioning. A child's collected experiences of interactions with others leave plenty of idealized images of self and others that fail to become fully differentiated. Such images are idealized because they ignore contradictory ('bad') dimensions of the self or the other that contradict the 'goodness' around which the fledgling psyche needs to organize itself. The fusion of idealized self and idealized other operates as a cultural imperative: If I am not a certain way, I am not at all (or I will experience such anxiety that I would rather not be at all). Put simply, by doing the things one is supposed to do, one avoids being what one should not be. The idealized images that guide behaviour positively in this way usually operate in conjunction with sets of *fused* negatively toned self/other images linked to aggressive and other unacceptable impulses. The power of ideals comes from this linkage. Again, the lack of differentiation between unconscious images of self and others makes it difficult to stand back from one's behaviour and to reflect on alternative courses of action.

In summary, the articulations of the psyche that determine personality styles develop as the result of internalized interpersonal regularities in the child's lifeworld. These can be referred to as *interaction paradigms* (Lorenzer 1976). In every case these can be described in terms of a subject pole (self) and object pole (other) and an emotional bond between these poles (Kernberg 1977). As we have seen, interaction paradigms can be characterized in two ways: by greater or lesser differentiation of self from other and by the degree of ambivalence achieved in either images of self or other. Interaction paradigms can also be analysed in terms of the affective valences associated with either pole and with the paradigm as a whole. In fact, as a child develops towards adulthood, a major task is to move through a series of extrapolations on the basic positive/negative structure to develop capacities for a wide range of feelings: guilt, shame, authority, doubt, irony, scepticism, nostalgia, respect, and so on.

A second look at this list of emotions will quickly convince one that, to a large degree, the determination of initial positive or negative qualities and their elabouration is a cultural affair, mediated by the socializing institutions experienced in childhood. In other words, each cultural system has its ways of training children to feel and understand a certain set of emotions that they will use to manoeuvre through the social world. Each culture defines the goodness and badness of feelings and associated behaviours in slightly different ways. Each child receives this package with a slightly different twist, due to idiosyncrasies of early experience, caretakers, regional cultural variations, social class, and so forth. Then, on the basis of this package, and often in reaction to it, the young person begins a long process of trying on roles through processes of *identification*. Core representations of self and other shape the development of ambitions and ideals in relation to talents and skills (Alford 1991). At first this is done through play; later, much more seriously – or at least, with more serious consequences. The search is never completed for each role evolves into new ones and with each role change the basic emotional structure that formed in early life strains to accommodate to the demands of social expectations. When this is not possible, role boundaries get stretched or violated and new roles are adopted or invented.

The distinction between the core of the psyche and the roles that one adopts over the life course is crucial. It will provide the key dimensions along which we may examine claims to the effect that modernity has had a significant impact on human personality. It is easy enough to demonstrate that modernization changes what people do. Our question has to do with changes that might be occurring in the underlying psychological structures and styles that we bring to bear on what we do.

DIFFERENCES IN STRUCTURE AND STYLE

An individual's psychological structure and style tend to be manifested in interaction with others so consistently that even in non-scientific circles we begin to think in terms of types of persons or personalities. In everyday language we have names for these types: for example, a person might be shy, outgoing, aggressive, creative, impulsive, dull or ambitious. Most of these types can be accounted for by referring to an organization of internalized object relations, of representations of self and others, that predisposes the individual to interpret the world of others in a particular way and to act fairly consistently in conjunction with that interpretation. For example, the object-relational schemas of the aggressive person may be such that other people are experienced as withholding and uncaring. Whether they actually are so is of little importance. The aggressive person's interpretations of others lead him or her to forceful and domineering actions. In response, others are likely to behave in ways that are actually withholding or rejecting. Thus, the cycle continues.

Implicit in most of the labels available for describing types of persons is a social evaluation that varies according to context. In contexts such as sports and war, the aggressive person is valued; in friendship and academia, less so. Scientific personality psychology has pushed the idea that there are simply different types of persons and that these differences are either inherited and/or learned so early that they are hard to change. No particular type is inherently more desirable that any other. Desirability depends on context. The process of social evaluation comes after the fact and although it shapes outward behaviour – for example, by teaching aggressive persons to keep their aggressiveness in check if they wish to get what they want – it does not change structure or style as I have described them. This point of view logically leads to the contemporary emphases on social skills training and behavioural self-management for those who happen to fall into unpopular personality types.

This seemingly generous point of view is mistaken. Its attempt at egalitarian relativism not only sidesteps complex psychological, cultural and ethical issues but in fact could be seen as an abdication of social responsibility. As the first part of this chapter insists, the psyche is structured and styled in interaction with others. The structures and styles that are established in childhood are not merely combinations of randomly distributed traits. Instead, they are different *capacities for relatedness* – for empathy, self-understanding, trustworthiness, constructive expression and communication of feelings, and other capacities that make intimacy, friendship and caring possible. These capacities are also related to the enjoyment of life in general and the qualities of meaningfulness that are available to a person. To value such capacities is, of course, a value choice, a culturally and historically mediated choice. There have been times and places in which brutality or stoic self-sufficiency have instead been favoured traits. I make my own concerns explicit here because many models of human development have claimed to be value free and cross-culturally valid when in fact they were, for example, phallocentric or ethnocentric. In emphasizing capacities for relatedness, I am highlighting a theme that runs through the object-relations model of development as well as preparing the ground for part of my primary argument about the impact of modernity on the psyche.

If we begin with an explicit emphasis on capacities for relatedness as a primary *telos* of psychological development, a notion of what is less than desirable development can be established, and, as the literature of psychoanalysis demonstrates, a rich vocabulary for psychopathology can be elabourated to describe different forms of less than desirable development. These forms are nothing more than different structures and styles of the psyche.

In the following sketch of a model of psychopathology we will refer to the two primary dimensions of psychological development highlighted in the first part of this chapter as *self–other differentiation* and *de-idealization*, the establishment of ambivalent images of self and other. Capacities for relatedness depend upon adequate development along each of these dimensions. Although the two processes are interwoven, they can be considered separately in order to isolate specific problems related to each.

Adequate self–other differentiation involves the gradual defusion of self-representations and associated feelings from representations of others. Progress on this dimension is often referred to in developmental theory as separation-individuation. As noted earlier, the process can be facilitated by experiences with trustworthy caretakers who understand the child's varying needs for comfort and space. It can be hindered by anxiety-provoking separateness related to neglect or by intrusive overinvolvement in the child's space. Inadequate self–other differentiation manifests itself in various ways. Personality disorders such as the dependent, the paranoid and the narcissistic reflect attempts to manage inadequate self–other differentiation. At higher levels of functioning, problems on this dimension of development can show up in difficulties with commitment, susceptibility to peer pressure, sexual inhibitions, incapacity to be alone, feelings of emptiness, excessive guilt, showing off, and other traits that signify both fear of self-assertion as well as false autonomy.

The process of de-idealization allows the originally tentative self to tolerate perceptions of defects and discomforting affect in others as well as in the self. Prior to the development of this capacity the experience of self tends to be organized around all-good representations of the other as loving, perfect and wonderful. By banking on idealized images of others the self preserves an infantile sense of omnipotence. At first, this serves an important function in managing anxiety and powerful affects that might threaten the fragile core of the self. Later, however, such affective splitting of self- and other-representations into all good and all bad becomes a severe hindrance to reality testing. Progress beyond this point is nevertheless difficult because it requires a capacity to give up idealized images of self and others and to tolerate imperfections in both self and others. Because of the letdown associated with de-idealization, Melanie Klein (Klein 1935) even speaks of the stage it sets up as the 'depressive position'. Those whose childhood environments do not facilitate the passage of the psyche into the de-idealized stage are likely to be intolerant of imperfection and prone to brief infatuations followed by sudden devaluation and rejection of others. They may also struggle with a sense of victimization or persecution, and entertain various fantasies of omnipotent control over their world (Kroll 1988; Kernberg 1985).

Self–other differentiation and de-idealization are only two of the primary dimensions along which capacities for relatedness develop. Authors such as Greenspan point to these dimensions as the primary ones involved in accounting for what are known as *borderline* psychopathology. Referring to self–other differentiation as 'representational differentiation', Greenspan writes:

> Most borderline individuals evidence their major problems in the area of representational differentiation. There is often not a complete deficit, but a lack of stability in the differentiation of self/nonself. At times of stress, for example, there is confusion as to what is their feeling and what is someone else's feeling. There may be disruptions in the capacity for impulse control, the sense of a 'me' acting on a 'you' becomes temporarily confused as part of an intense feeling state involving passion, rage, severe separation anxiety, or loss.
>
> (Greenspan 1989: 276)

De-idealization is explained in Greenspan's work in terms of 'thematic-affective differentiation', a capacity which he also links to borderline pathology:

> [S]ome individuals can behave in a highly differentiated way when it comes to competitiveness, anger, and assertiveness. At work, where these themes dominate, they perform admirably well. They compete effectively with other people, feel organized during states of competition, and have no difficulty at these times in sensing who they are and who other people are. When they come home, however, and deal with dependency, sexuality, and pleasure, they may have a sense of 'losing my boundaries'. They are frequently unsure of what they are thinking and what the other person is thinking. They easily feel rejected and hurt. They go into reactive rages secondary to problems around dependency and pleasure.
>
> (Greenspan 1989: 277–278)

I have highlighted the linkage between developmental deficits and borderline pathology because this connection puts teeth into the contemporary argument that social conditions in industrialized societies of the late twentieth century are systematically producing borderline personality structures and styles. This argument is also related to the more frequent diagnosis of both modern culture and personalities as narcissistic – an issue to which we return in subsequent chapters. Now that we are armed with a more articulated perspective on the psyche, I turn afresh to the thorny problem of establishing linkages between the modern social system and the formation or, should we say, deformation, of the psyche.

Chapter 5

The domination of desire

My inquiry thus far has articulated two domains: the colonization of the lifeworld that accompanies capitalist modernization and the formation of the psyche in early socialization processes. In relation to the first domain, I have argued that Habermas's conceptualization of modernization provides both essential sociological concepts and fruitful hypotheses regarding the sources of modern social pathologies. Specifically, Habermas shows how capitalist modernization thrives on cognitive-instrumental forms of rationality that disrupt the meaning-sustaining processes of the lifeworld. In connection with the second domain, I laid out a model of personality development grounded in psychoanalytic object relations theory. This model suggests that the experience of meaningfulness and capacities for relatedness depend on a complex process of psychic structuration in early childhood. Now, the challenge is to work out a useful way of combining these theoretical frameworks in order to clarify the impact of capitalist modernization on the formation of the psyche.

In my review of Schneider's *Neurosis and Civilization* (1975) in Chapter 2, I illustrated some pitfalls in theoretical analyses that combine psychoanalytic psychology and Marxist social theory. An apparent incompatibility at the level of basic assumptions tends to produce contradictions in whatever syntheses are proposed (cf. Robinson 1969; Castilla del Pino 1969; Lichtman 1982; Chasseguet-Smirgel and Grunberger 1986; Frosh 1987; Tolman 1994). For example, psychoanalysis emphasizes intrapsychic sources of motivation while Marxism looks to social structure in its accounts of social behaviour. Marxist approaches tend to emphasize actors' capacities for rational action, while psychoanalysis primarily documents the obstacles to rationality. Despite such theoretical challenges, the insights of Freud and Marx continue to inspire very provocative interpretations of contemporary experience based on syntheses of the two perspectives (cf. Brown 1973; Kaës 1980; Kovel 1981; Kodai 1984; Whitebook 1985; Allingham 1987; Alford 1989; Benjamin 1988; Craib 1990; Zizek 1989, 1991; Earnest 1992). A few of the challenges encountered in such endeavours will be noted, if not resolved, in the following discussion.

REPRESSION IN THE AFFLUENT SOCIETY

The current horizons of thought at the intersection of psychoanalysis and critical social theory were established in the 1960s by Herbert Marcuse (1899–1979), a primary collaborator with the Frankfurt Institute of Social Research (cf. Jay 1973). His work has yet to be surpassed for its clarity of perception and originality as well as the power of its implications. Developing themes explored simplistically by the controversial Wilhelm Reich, Marcuse weaves together insights from psychoanalysis, existential phenomenology, and Hegelian Marxism in an analysis of ideology and personality in advanced industrial societies. Although Marcuse's analyses predate Habermas's work by some ten to twenty years, they are especially rich in psychological insights related to the colonization of the lifeworld. Nevertheless, Marcuse's perspective requires some revision. In light of Habermas's framework and psychoanalytic object relations theory, I will show how this can be done in relation to Marcuse's critique of instrumental rationality. I will also argue that some of Marcuse's emphases need to be retained to correct for Habermas's overly cognitive orientation.

Much of the power in Marcuse's outlook stems from the fact that he affirms the most controversial components of Freud's theory: the notion of infantile sexuality, the opposition of the life and death instincts, the primacy of repressed unconscious in psychic life, and the fundamental antagonism between individual and society. He criticizes humanistic psychologists, such as Erich Fromm, for diluting Freud's revolutionary principles, such as the idea that consciousness is an outgrowth of the instinctual drives, in order to present a more benign picture of human nature (Marcuse 1962, 1970; Jacoby 1975; Elliott 1993).

Building on a basic principle of Marx's historical materialism, Marcuse introduces a historical perspective into Freud's portrayal of the conflictual relationship between the individual's instinctual desires and the requirements of society. In 'Civilization and its discontents', Freud (1930) had argued that the conflict between drives and the needs of society was universal and necessary. The repression of instinctual drives produces unhappiness and neurosis. Such suffering would always be the price we have to pay for civilization. Social stability and progress, in Freud's view, would always require the delay of gratification, the subjection of the pleasure principle to the reality principle.

In *Eros and Civilization*, Marcuse (1962) argued instead that neurosis and everyday unhappiness are best interpreted as the products of specific historical (and much more recent) developments. Repression represents an *internalization of domination* by external masters. It only became necessary historically in the stage of societal development – linked to urbanization and industrialization when external force and overt policing of human behaviour became impractical. The internal agency that organizes psychic repression, misrepresented as a universal psychological structure in Freud's notion of the superego, works as an agent of the ultimate social authority (the king, the master, etc.). The family and the Church collaborated in the establishment of this controlling agency in new generations as a means to retaining institutional power.

Echoing Horkheimer and Adorno's (1948/1982) thesis on the dialectic of the Enlightenment, Marcuse described how the emergence of modern subjectivity (in what Habermas treats as the differentiation of the personality component of the lifeworld) also opened up the space in which the 'inner self' or ego could become an object of cognitive-instrumental manipulation. In other words, individuals were positioned to view their personal experience and behaviour as objects that could be subjected to control, planning and ordering in the interest of social success. Social ideals associated with the Enlightenment, such as self-control and rational action, were internalized as idealized self-images and began to operate at the psychic level by inhibiting affect and impulsive behaviour related to the erotic and destructive drives. This move towards self-control is one of the original meanings of the term 'civilization' (Kuzmics 1984). Such were the origins of the bourgeois superego so extensively documented by Freud.

Marcuse (1962, 1964, 1970) proposes that this basic structure of the modern psyche changed dramatically in the advanced industrial societies of the post-war Western world. A curious reversal occurred in these societies when material scarcity was for the most part abolished. Scarcity had previously always been the material basis for the victory of the reality principle over the pleasure principle. A certain amount of work had always needed to be done in order to survive. Instinctual gratification and basic life pleasures had to be renounced or at least delayed until old age or the afterlife. But, Marcuse wondered, what happens when the basic survival needs of individuals in advanced industrial society are met by increasingly automated industrial and agricultural production systems? Why should people keep working?

Although such questions are still premature for the majority of the earth's inhabitants who still struggle to meet daily needs – roughly four billion people – it is likely that these issues will become more widely relevant as capitalist industrialization encompasses the globe under the auspices of the 'new world order'.

Marcuse introduced two concepts to describe the psychological situation of the individuals in affluent society. The first, *surplus repression*, refers to the amount of instinctual renunciation that a society requires above and beyond that necessary to maintain social order and to meet basic survival needs. This extra repression mirrors the surplus value or profits created for capitalists by workers who are underpaid for their labour. As a result of surplus repression, people are willing to work much more than is objectively necessary. They work to meet false needs fabricated by advertisements in order to keep the productive system and the economic order from collapsing. They may have more material comfort than any prior civilization has provided to its citizens, but are so enslaved psychologically that they have little time or aesthetic capacity to enjoy the benefits of 'progress' and economic growth.

A second notion, the *performance principle*, is also relevant here. This is Marcuse's term for the continuous, irrational demand for output from workers in modern society. In contrast, Freud's reality principle allowed one to quit when basic needs were met. The performance principle arises in advanced capitalism because the economic system must stimulate continuous consumption and production. Under the reign of the performance principle, even leisure time is filled with 'business' (busyness) and is dedicated to competition with oneself or others, vicarious competition through spectator sports or compulsive buying.

As an alternative to this irrational society, Marcuse hoped for a 'sensuous' order in which work and play would be fused and in which the overdevelopment of the West would be halted in order to achieve a redistribution of resources to meet the basic needs of all the earth's inhabitants. He was pessimistic regarding the achievement of these goals, but he did see some grounds for hope. Marcuse's pessimism is obvious in *One-dimensional Man* (1964), for example, where he admitted that the groups historically positioned to bring about dramatic social change, the working classes of the Western industrial societies, had been integrated into the capitalist system by material prosperity to such a degree that they no longer sensed the need for change. Their consciousness reflected the reality of the system in which they had been produced as individuals: life was meant for self-gratification through material consumption. In a sense, there was only 'one dimension' in which to live and function: that of the bureaucratically managed consumer society backed by and supporting a military–industrial complex.

At a certain point in its development, this social system could even afford to loosen previous restrictions on sexual gratification, as perhaps demonstrated by the so-called sexual revolution of the 1960s and 1970s. Marcuse felt that this sexual freedom had the effect of attaching people even more strongly to the social order that permitted such a variety of pleasures. He coined the term *repressive desublimation* to describe this undoing of the cultural system that had previously required the repression and sublimation of erotic desire into socially valued activities. This desublimation is labelled 'repressive' because, by affording more direct sensuous gratification, the system was spared challenges to its stability.

The repression of the working classes, who might otherwise seek to overcome inequalities in the distribution of wealth, was thus maintained. People who are well fed, sexually satiated and fascinated by fancy technological toys are not likely to rebel against the system that takes such good care of them. With only minor resentment, they are even willing to work at boring and pointless jobs in order to maintain their status in such a system. They are further enslaved by the fact that their primary images of the good life are supplied by advertising departments in the first place. Vague memories of non-consumerist modes of contentedness – simple picnics, playing with the kids, learning to play an instrument, reading a good book, a chat with the neighbours – stand little chance against bright, catchy, eroticized advertisements for new products. Paradoxically, Marcuse points out, the sexual revolution unleashed by repressive desublimation actually engendered a narrowing of sexuality into genitally focused performances that mirrored production processes at work.

This point deserves further consideration. Some will wonder how Marcuse could be critical of such a successful social system. Certainly its subjects are not complaining much. Marcuse would reply, without forgetting to mention the glaring fact that this abundance was achieved and is maintained largely at the expense of the masses in the developing nations – through imperialism, exploitation of natural resources and cheap labour, cultural domination, and so forth – that the psychological configuration of the individual in consumer society must be contrasted with available ideals, for example, the humanistic ideals of the Enlightenment. Those ideals portrayed a self-reflective and socially aware subject meaningfully engaged in a fully democratic society.

Modern mass individuals, as Marcuse diagnosed them, have little capacity for making autonomous value judgements. Their choices are made automatically by an ego that merely mimics the contrived reality of consumer society. This very weak ego constantly seeks assurances of its worth. Persons who suffer even a minor blow to their self-esteem know just what to do: Buy something! Buying things makes you feel good! Eat something sweet and tasty! Drink something! Get drunk! Get high! Make love! Watch a pornographic movie! . . . These remedies bring only temporary relief – if they satisfy at all – with the consequence that the entire society gets caught up in a vicious cycle of mood-manipulating consumption and production, both ends of which are managed quite consciously, and cynically, by profit-makers using the most advanced advertising and market research technologies. Given this social environment, it is not surprising that over the past few decades major psychological syndromes have developed around eating and addictive behaviours as well as compulsive shopping or shoplifting.

For these reasons, Marcuse was pessimistic about the possibility that social change would be brought about by the working or middle classes in consumer society. He recognized, however, the potential of groups that had not yet been fully integrated into the system. Assessing the situation in the United States, in the 1960s, he thought students and ethnic minorities were most likely to create an effective counterculture since they were marginal to or excluded from economic and political power (Marcuse 1969). Furthermore, these groups had not yet succumbed to the spell of the system. At the global level, Marcuse perceived that the Third World nations might still find ways to avoid integration into either state socialism or corporate capitalism. Given the contemporary disarray of student and minority rights movements, and the painful experience of Third World nations such as Nicaragua that have tried to find a third path, it would seem that Marcuse's pessimism was still too optimistic.

GROUNDS FOR RESISTANCE

Some of Marcuse's most interesting psychological theorizing addressed the question of how an interest in resistance to the one-dimensional system might be maintained by subjects who have been nearly totally co-opted. It is here that a re-reading can be attempted in light of Habermas and object-relations theory. Marcuse first notes that memory preserves images of free and total gratification experienced in early life. This would correspond to basic internalized interaction paradigms characterized by self–other reciprocity or mutuality and might comprise both fused, idealized images of self and other as well as differentiated, less idealized images. These psychological structures constitute an emotional foundation for images of freedom and real happiness to stand in contrast with what individuals encounter in the routine drudgery and pseudogratification of everyday life in adulthood. Resistance to the one-dimensional system might thus be fuelled by a sense that key promises in life have been betrayed.

In a related process, images shaped by the neglected or excluded pleasure principle intrude into the oppressed consciousness through fantasy and daydreaming: 'the unconscious, the deepest and oldest layer of the mental personality, is the drive for integral gratification, which is the absence of want and repression' (Marcuse 1962: 17). Marcuse hypothesized that in a society with less social and psychological repression, the life instincts would win out over the destructive instincts. The performance principle would create the conditions for its own demise. Meanwhile, the life instincts would give rise to fantasies of an ideal world, such as those expressed in authentic artistic creations (Marcuse 1978). These images assert claims for an aesthetic–natural–erotic environment, for a merger of technology and art. Perhaps we are beginning to see some of Marcuse's hopes fulfilled in some of the programmes of the ecology movement. In any case, among major twentieth-century social theorists, it was Marcuse who most fully glimpsed the fact that, in another paradox of the dialectic, Nature itself – a sphere of external reality savagely dominated by men throughout the course of history – would be the last reservoir of inspiration for the liberation of humankind when the yoke of its own modern institutions became too oppressive. How ironic that recognizing the degradation of external nature has been easier than perceiving the domination of inner human nature.

In Marcuse's work we again see the fundamental role played by symbolic and cultural processes in determining the quality of individual life. What he refers to as one-dimensionality at the level of culture, society and personality could be understood in Habermasian terms as resulting from the colonization of the lifeworld by cognitive-instrumental rationality. This levelling sets up a widespread failure to sustain communicative action against the backdrop of a symbolic lifeworld. In the personality component of the lifeworld individuals are left to construct identities on the basis of objectifying forms of self-interpretation and lack capacity for the sorts of intersubjective communication that Habermas sees as the foundation for meaningful participation in a democratic social order.

The role of the instinctual drives in motivating resistance is crucial for Marcuse. This has been the issue around which many have parted company with his perspective. It is generally argued that to speak of drives is to posit a fixed human nature, a move that quickly leads to conservative positions, for example, that since humankind is selfish and competitive by nature it is pointless to push for equality or peace. But for Marcuse, 'whatever formations of repression come to predominate in society, the existence of the instinctual realm indicates that an alternative, personal core of selfhood always remains, timelessly residing in the unconscious' (Elliott 1993: 507–508). I will not dwell on this issue, but I will mention that recent interpretations of Freud's concept of unconscious drives, particularly the death instinct, emphasize their role in sustaining imaginative, symbolic processes (Boothby 1991; Elliott 1992). The difference between Marcuse's view and these analyses is that Marcuse tended not to differentiate between biological instincts and their 'drive' derivatives in the psyche. The instincts are seen as static and universal whereas their psychic derivatives are regarded as the site of flux and symbolic shifting. Marcuse's equation of instincts with their derivatives pushed him into an unnecessarily deterministic position on human nature.

As mentioned earlier, Marcuse emphasized artistic and sensuous experience as the means for countering self-objectifying attitudes. This means he hoped that spontaneous aesthetic–expressive rationality grounded in the erotic drives would undermine the reification fostered by the system. Habermas would point out, as he does in a critique of Adorno, that Marcuse should also have looked to the balancing effect of moral–practical rationality, particularly for its potential to ground challenges to the social order in norms shared by other members of society, many of which are already encoded in formal law or in declarations of human rights (Habermas 1984).

Habermas would also argue that Marcuse overestimated the degree to which the lifeworld is colonized by the system. By attending mostly to the processes of social administration and cultural production as they affect adult lifestyles, Marcuse overlooked at least one major area in which the symbolic reproduction of the lifeworld had not yet been totally disrupted. I discuss this oversight in the next section.

FAMILY AS CORPORATE AGENT

A major shortcoming in Marcuse's analysis of the psychological conse-quences of capitalist modernization stems from insufficient attention to the processes of socialization that produce the personality styles he criti-cizes. He speaks as if the adult experience of one-dimensionality is enough to produce one-dimensional personalities. In this regard his work is simi-lar to the social psychological approach of Inkeles (1983), or the pheno-menological sociology of Berger, Berger, and Kellner (1974), in that it points to parallel processes at psychological and social levels and does not establish the mediations or mechanisms through which such substantial psychological transformations might be effected. For example, we saw in Chapter 2 that Berger, Berger and Kellner assumed that life in bureau-cratic organizations induces bureaucratic forms of consciousness that are, in turn, transferred into other life spheres, for example, into planning intimate relationships. While it may be the case that people begin to order their private lives in a manner similar to the way they handle office matters, one cannot assume that this represents a change in personality structure or style resulting from life in modern institutions.

The psychoanalyst Kernberg concurs with the position that macrosocial and cultural change does not, in and of itself, foster changes in personality structures. For such changes to occur, he argues, there would also have to be major changes in the ways that families raise their children in their early years (Kernberg 1975: 223). Hence, as compelling as Marcuse's descriptive diagnosis may be, it does not help us much in deciding whether capitalist modernization is actually connected causally with the pathology he describes. This theoretical gap is not uncommon. Thomson (1989) suggests that many authors err in their studies of social change because they simply reorganize concepts 'in the air' with little connection to the actual experience of modern subjects or do not attend to mediating processes between society and psyche. As we continue to discover in the course of this inquiry, however, a solid path to take us beyond speculation is hard to find.

Certain authors influenced by Marx and Freud have managed to pay more attention to the mechanisms of personality formation under capitalism, particularly to the role of the family as an agent of the political economy. Unfortunately, their analyses are limited for other reasons. In Chapter 2, we noted how Schneider's analysis bogged down in its allegiance to orthodox Freudian concepts. Wilhelm Reich's innovative early work was too devoted to the orthodox concepts of both psychoanalysis and Marxism, leading to a reductionistic materialism. Erich Fromm certainly placed plenty of emphasis on the family's role in socialization, but underestimated the ability of capitalist institutions to shape behaviour away from meeting our existential needs for relatedness, transcendence, rootedness, identity, and a frame of orientation and devotion (Fromm 1947, 1955). Finally, the pathbreaking empirical work reported in *The Authoritarian Personality* (Adorno *et al.* 1950) established important linkages between psychopathology and the class positions of families, but, because of then prevalent constraints on academic freedom, the authors chose not to spell out their critique of capitalist class society.

Rather than dwell on extended critiques of such authors, I have chosen to elaborate what I see as one of most intriguing attempts to analyse the impact of capitalist modernization on socialization. This perspective has its roots in the work of Adorno and Marcuse and is especially significant because it begins to account for the impact of transformations of family structure in the type of social order that is rapidly becoming the global norm, that is, corporate capitalism.

It may have been clear to some readers from the outset that our attention in this book could be focused primarily on the impact of modernization on early socialization processes, particularly in families, but also in schools and other socializing institutions. In part, I avoided an earlier introduction of the family context because the dominant tendency in psychology is to analyse the functioning of families apart from social and historical contexts. For example, in studies of child development the nuclear family is often taken as the norm or the ideal, when it is actually a relatively new phenomenon in human history and appears to be increasingly atypical as the twentieth century winds down. Families do, however, retain a certain degree of autonomy from direct determination by sociohistorical processes, particularly in the ways they exercise their function as socializing agents, and for this reason alone one needs a general sense of how families have been affected by modernization and whether these changes can be linked to the production of different personality structures or styles.

The issue of tracing changes in the effects of family life is a complex one. In his *Critical Theory of the Family*, Poster explains why:

> It may be that the structure of the family is so dependent on other
> levels of society (the state or the economy) that changes in its structure

cannot be understood through reference to aspects of the family itself. It may be that the structure of the family is wholly determined by the economy or politics. However, there are important theoretical reasons for doubting this conclusion. Just as political forms do not emerge in lockstep with economic forms, so family forms are not perfectly contemporaneous with other levels of society. Industrial capitalism and representative democracy, for example, do not emerge at the same time as modern family forms. Therefore the family enjoys partial autonomy from the state and the economy.

(Poster 1978: 141)

This partial autonomy of the family makes it difficult to link social change to changes in family structure. Because of time-lags, regional and subcultural differences, and a multitude of other variables, one never can be sure what it is at the social level that is becoming manifest at the level of the family. Empirical research conducted by Al-Haj (1988), for example, shows that modernization effects tend to be confounded by socio-demographic and cultural variables. Studies by Stewart and Healy (1989) reveal important cohort effects in social change processes. So, to link social change to specific psychological effects brought about through the mediation of the family would be especially challenging. Given these analytic problems, can anything valid be said about the impact of modernization on the family?

In the context of this inquiry it is worth a try, for, as Poster argues, it is exactly through its impact on the structure of the psyche and early identity development that the family exercises its primary function as a socializing agent:

[T]o develop categories of family structure that account for a wide diversity of social definitions and for the coherence and uniqueness of family experience, the theory of the family must turn to the psychological level and develop categories which permit the understanding of vastly divergent family structures in terms of their emotional pattern. The family is thus the place where the psychic structure is formed and where experience is characterized in the first instance by emotional patterns.

(Poster 1978: 143)

I will show that this task is even harder than it appears, but it has to be attempted in order to uncover a more fundamental obstacle to this sort of analysis.

First, we can adopt a useful general framework bearing on the social situation of the family from Luke's interesting book *Screens of Power* (1989). Luke's analysis draws on the work of Lasch (1977), Zaretsky (1976) and Baudrillard (1981) in a description of changes in the function of the family associated with the shift from entrepreneurial to corporate capitalism in Europe and North America.

As we saw in Chapter 3, entrepreneurial capitalism stimulated the spread of rationalized production systems and related economic and social institutions into geographical regions still dominated by feudal arrangements. Production for local use was gradually replaced by production of commodities for exchange. This change had effects beyond the marketplace. Luke summarizes these developments:

> As this exchange-based logic of commodification generated in the workingplace penetrated the private living space, the city penetrated the countryside, the market dominated the farm, the mind-worker subordinated the hand-worker, and the capitalist metropole imperialized the precapitalist periphery. With the advancement of this process, the bourgeois family system formed to cushion members against the ravages of commodity exchange relations. In particular, women and children were slowly taken out of productive economic activity and put more into the domestic reproductive sphere of creating and maintaining the emotional haven of the household.
>
> (Luke 1989: 102)

The new bourgeois family structure, also known as the nuclear family, displaced extended family systems of various sorts and fostered the development of a self-reliant, future-oriented personality suited to the culture of entrepreneurial capitalism.

> To accumulate capital and to preserve themselves for production, bourgeois families, in turn, developed new social rituals for self-discipline, delayed satisfaction, and material sacrifice. Only in the privacy of the home and under strict rules of propriety could psychic, physical, and emotional needs be gratified, but just to the point of not weakening one's productivity by excess. Building up one's business, career, or estate demanded frugal discipline, and the child-centered family virtually transmuted the child into a market 'future' whose character had to be properly managed and invested in so that the child might also become productive.
>
> (Luke 1989: 104)

In this scenario we may note that the experience of the bourgeois family was always deeply penetrated by the contradictions of the capitalist economic order. With automation, craft work became devalued. Women's housework and emotional work with children were simultaneously idealized and trivialized. In the privacy of the home, patriarchal brutality and sexual frustration were kept from public view as the ideal of the family was propagandized in the budding mass media. Meanwhile, the miserable situation of the new urban working classes was improving all too slowly.

Most of these changes can be interpreted in Habermas's terms as related to the uncoupling of system and lifeworld.

By the late 1800s the era of expansive entrepreneurial capitalism was ending in Western Europe and North America. Certain limits were being reached. The industrializing nations had subdivided the precapitalist world into colonial empires. The latter provided raw materials but did not yet serve as vast markets for industrial products. 'Extensive' capitalist expansion was thus gradually replaced by 'intensive capitalist administration' (Luke 1989: 107). This strategy stressed the development of internal markets and the manipulation of demand through a further extension of instrumental rationality into the operations of the market and the state. The era of *corporate capitalism* was born:

> By mobilizing scientific research to technically inform and managerially guide industrial production, the entrepreneurs slowly concentrated their market shares and capital holdings through oligopolistic organization into large capital combines that could obviate market forces by creating a planned system of production. *Intensive* capitalist administration, with a new stress on organization, consummativity, and managing the 'demand' side of industry, presented itself as the most rational path out of the tangled maze of entrepreneurial capital's limits.
>
> (Luke 1989: 107)

The shift from entrepreneurial to corporate capitalism may seem far afield from processes that might affect the family, but as Luke points out, the family represented the next backward region that needed to be colonized and subjected to instrumental rationality in the interest of capitalist accumulation.

THE DECLINE OF THE BOURGEOIS FATHER

With this historical perspective in mind, one can look more closely at how the transition from entrepreneurial to corporate capitalism might have influenced socialization processes.

In both Habermas and Marcuse one finds references to a gradual shift from 'autonomous' moral development within the family to a more direct mediation of personal values and ideals by imperatives of the social system. Both authors are banking on earlier studies of German families conducted by fellow Frankfurt School members Horkheimer and Adorno (Institute of Social Research 1936; cf. Jay 1973; Held 1980). They traced the shift just mentioned, from personal autonomy to manipulation by the system, to socially produced changes in family life. The reproduction of the institutions and culture of liberal society in the era of entrepreneurial capitalism had depended on the authority and agency of bourgeois fathers in the socialization of children.

In this ideal(ized) bourgeois nuclear family, the child experienced the tender love of the mother and the firm discipline of the father, who having carefully thought through his own place in the world, would be best positioned to inculcate appropriate values and behaviour in the child. The lifeworld he hoped to transmit would have entailed both traditional assumptions stemming from religious and political ideology as well as elements of critical rationality of the sort developed in scientific and technical circles. For the bourgeois father, cultural meanings, personal identity and social solidarity were fairly intact.

Interactions with the bourgeois father provoked the various forms of the Oedipus complex catalogued by Freud. The complex was to be resolved (by males) through identification with the father and an internalization of his particular values. The child could later enter the world with a set of values and ideals shaped in the relatively autonomous realm of the home. If the young adult found the world to fall short of these ideals, a continuation of the Oedipal rebellion combined with a displaced search for primary oneness with the mother would trigger criticism of social institutions and revolt, if necessary, to bring about necessary social transformations (Held 1980).

Adorno and Marcuse both argue that this arrangement ran into trouble when the contradictions of capitalist development in Europe undermined the autonomy of bourgeois fathers in the early twentieth century. Instead of preserving their pride as public citizens, businessmen and heads of households, they or their sons found themselves increasingly reduced to positions of dependency in bureaucratic welfare states in the ranks of civil servants, factory workers or the unemployed. Their authority in the home declined analogously. Adorno (1951/1982) traced the psychological roots of Fascism to this decline: the weakened father needed a powerful father-figure to boost his own flagging self-worth.

The consequences for socialization, according to the decline-of-the-father hypothesis, were equally grave. The values of the father had provided a shield and a filter against the rising power of mass propaganda, but in the absence of the father's powerful symbolic figure in the early life of the child, values of the newly emerging 'bureaucratic society of manipulated consumption' (Brown 1973) were broadcast directly into the home sphere with the help of new technologies such as radio and other mass propaganda. Early personality formation began to be mediated less by the vicissitudes of the Oedipus complex and more by exposure to whatever happened to be broadcast for public consumption. In Habermas's terms, the personality component of the lifeworld and the socialization processes associated with its reproduction were increasingly subjected to the means–ends logic of instrumental rationality, displacing modes of communication through which alternative conceptions of a good life might have been formed. At the level of object relations, this would tend to be reflected in rigid and objectifying conceptions of self in relation to others and a related inability to tolerate ambivalence and complex emotional states – a style not unlike what is known as the authoritarian personality.

Besides its circumscribed relevance, this intriguing example of how one might examine contemporary family dynamics is flawed for several reasons. First, it is not likely that authoritarian discipline is essential to the establishment of critical self-reflection and autonomous judgement (Benjamin 1977). In fact, Adorno *et al.* (1950) link harsh discipline to cognitive rigidity, prejudice and antidemocratic attitudes. Second, this analysis focuses on the parents' overt behaviour and ignores its symbolic dimensions. As Elliott points out:

> Marcuse and Adorno view the decline of the *real father's* social prestige as inevitably bringing with it a disintegration of moral conscience and individual autonomy in the current social order. In psychoanalytic theory, however, the function of paternal authority in the Oedipus complex is principally *symbolic*: to bar the small child's desire towards the mother through introducing the structuring law of social relations, the prohibition of incest. This function, it should be emphasized, is not in any way dependent on the actual social or economic situation of the father.
>
> (Elliott 1993: 533)

I believe Elliott overstates the case only slightly. 'Real fathers' can, of course, behave in ways that affect their children's development. The impact of their behaviour is, however, always mediated by the symbolic resources available to the children at various stages of development. Children are never dealing just with their own fathers, but also with their own subjective, symbolic constructions of fatherhood in relation to culturally transmitted concepts and expectations. I would say, therefore, that if the decline of the prestige of the bourgeois father had any general effect, it would have derived from the complex interplay between symbolic representations of fatherhood at a cultural level and routine practices in the concrete activity of particular fathers (e.g. going into rages, withdrawing into their newspapers or hobbies, avoiding the home, etc.).

Finally, Elliott (1993) also points out that Marcuse and Adorno overlook the impact of pre-Oedipal development in which the role of the mother is typically more important. As we saw in Chapter 4, it is in the pre-Oedipal phase (years 1 to 3) that the psychological bases for autonomy and capacities for relatedness are established.

The decline-of-the-father thesis seems damaged by conceptual slippage between two domains: the actual socializing practices of parents with their children and the symbolic mediations of such practices by socio-cultural and subjective processes. Although one can separate the two realms analytically, in practice they always interpenetrate. A parent's nurturing action, for example, might be well appreciated by a young child, while the same act would be resented by her strident adolescent child. These acts also have different meanings from the parent's point of view.

At this advanced point, I must conclude that the Frankfurt School's basic line of argument regarding the impact of monopoly capitalism on the socialization process fails to be convincing. This means that I will have to recentre this inquiry and return afresh to my original question.

The destructive processes engendered by the contradictions of capitalist 'development' are obvious in world affairs, in environmental degradation, the ugly inequality and crass commercialism of our cities, homelessness, conspicuous consumption, interpersonal violence and the stupidity of most television entertainment. The destruction is less conspicuous, but even more disturbing, where we observe its psychological consequences in our families, friends and workmates and ourselves: unnecessary competitiveness, fragile self-esteem, consumerist binges, dehumanization, relationship problems, random and senseless lifestyle changes, conversions to reactionary worldviews, chemical dependency and scores of other symptoms of emotional damage commonly reported in psychocultural critiques of modern life (cf. Wachtel 1989; Cushman 1990). Can the destruction be linked to its source in a convincing manner?

Faced with this question, some social scientists would call for longitudinal, sociological and economic data on families, complete with psychological profiles based on clinical interviews. If such data could be gathered, it would be interesting, but relativists could argue that such studies would be inconclusive for they would merely document the characteristics of families in a particular period and place. They would also run into the same confounding of variables we noted in Chapter 2. A great deal of energy would be expended to make little headway in understanding the phenomena that need to be explained. Furthermore, I, for one, am not going to wait around while my well-intentioned colleagues in the behavioural sciences design and conduct such a study. The problems are too pressing and the level of suffering is intolerable.

I prefer to take a different tack, at the level of theory, picking up a cue from Habermas and others that the psychological destruction associated with capitalist modernization is produced by disruptions of the symbolic reproduction of the personality component of the lifeworld. Up to this point, I have repeatedly skipped lightly over the issue of what is meant here by 'symbolic'. Since the early Frankfurt School also failed to include the symbolic dimension sufficiently in its analyses of emotional life, I turn now to see if this shell can be cracked in a manner that contributes to the formulation of a generalizable strategy for social transformation.

Chapter 6

Ideological formations and their transcendence

My attempt to establish a linear path of causation leading from socio-economic order through social institutions and socializing processes to the formation of personality structures arrived at a dead end. Rather than establishing direct causal relations or even correlations between modernity and the psyche, this analytic strategy repeatedly unveiled the interwoven *symbolic* mediations of society's influences on the formation of personality. The simplistic billiard ball metaphor of social causation is obviously insufficient to grasp the web of discourses, values, practices and meanings in which individual subjectivity constructs and deconstructs itself. Fortunately, this dead end, which characterizes most social science conducted within an objectivistic epistemology, can be transcended without giving up the basic understandings we have already developed regarding the crisis of the modern psyche.

One could reason as follows: If the primary process through which modernization works its effects on the formation of the psyche is that described by Habermas as the colonization of the lifeworld, what is lacking in our inquiry thus far is a vocabulary for conceptualizing the sorts of lifeworld disruption that occur in the sphere of personality formation as a result of modernization. These effects would have to be distinguished from problems in personality formation that cannot be linked to macro-social processes. In other words, as we move away from an objectivistic analysis that ignored the symbolic mediations of personal experience, a set of terms referring to the systematic distortion of symbolic processes becomes necessary.

A term that links individual and society conceptually with particular attention to the symbolically mediated subjection of the individual to structures of economic and political power is *ideology*. In Marx's writings, ideology referred to ideas that supported the ruling class. The concept has been watered down to the point that it has come to denote any set of ideas, beliefs or values without regard to the interests they serve in relation to political and economic orders. In critical social theory, however, the concept of ideology retains its punch, but it is in need of a bit of dusting off and redefinition. Following the Frankfurt School, I will use the term to refer to a system of practices and representations that sustain social relations of domination, exploitation and oppression (Thompson 1984; Earnest 1992).

According to this definition, it is important to differentiate ideology from terms such as 'culture', 'worldview', 'set of attitudes' and 'belief system' that do not explicitly refer to power relations between subject and system. Ideology is often confused with these terms because it attempts to account for some of the same phenomena as they do and because it is also used to describe an orientation that is shared by many individuals and is not merely a private delusion. From the critical perspective, ideology can be distinguished clearly from other terms for its focus on *constraints* on self-understanding and intersubjectivity and the role that these constraints play in the stabilization of the social order and the maintenance of oppression and domination. These constraints usually involve a complex interaction of cognitive, affective and interpersonal action patterns. Bits and pieces of ideology are often described in isolation from their social function in terms of rationalization, denial, stereotyping, idealization, identification, reification, objectification, repression, projection, acting out, and so on.

It is important to note that most of the items in this list are psychological defences used to manage emotional conflict or reduce environmental complexity. At the individual level of analysis, such as that which is relevant to clinical work, the particular nature of the conflict managed by these defences would be of interest, but in *ideology criticism*, the aim is to unveil the manner in which the contradictory demands of social institutions mobilize defensive manoeuvres on the part of involved individuals, subjecting all participants to a form of life that is irrational, dehumanizing and unjust (Earnest 1992). Conceived in this manner, ideology criticism becomes essential to understanding what transpires in important life spheres, ranging from the workplace and the mass media to intimate relationships and artistic expression. In fact, the critique of ideology is the primary means by which certain questions left unanswered by Habermas can be addressed. For example, in a review and critique of Habermas's view of modernization, Thompson wonders:

> Why do members of the lifeworld *not* perceive that what they are threatened by is the uncontrolled growth of system complexity, rooted ultimately in the dynamics of capital accumulation and valorization? Why do they not resist this growth directly and demand, in an open and widespread way, the transformation of the economic system which underlies it?
>
> (Thompson 1984: 300)

In a similar fashion, Harvey (1985) concludes his study of the modern

urban consciousness with these questions: 'How can urbanized consciousness confront and tame the monstrous power of creative destruction
embodied in a capitalist mode of production?' 'How can political movements be mobilized that can confront the deep structure of class relations
that powers a capitalist mode of production?' (ibid.: 266). These sets of
questions beg for an analysis of ideological processes and they suggest
that an adequate view of modernity's impact on the psyche must describe
not only the consequences of domination, but also the means by which
its effects are maintained systemically and subjectively, as well as how
they might be overcome.

In the context of this inquiry, the psychosocial constraints to which
ideological processes subject modern individuals as they review their
possibilities and establish personal lifestyles are of most concern. In a
sense, this is a way of working backwards from features of individual
experience towards the macrosocial aspects of the colonization of the
lifeworld. The importance of this problem became apparent to me in my
research on self-deception in major life choices (Sloan 1987). In that
study of adult decision-making, I argued that both the practical and the
characterological contexts of life choices are structured by ideological
constraints. In each of the life histories reported in that book, an ideological dimension was apparent in the ways individuals went about resolving the dilemmas that set up transformations of their life structures
('turning points'). At first glance, it appeared that many of the participants
in the study were being 'decisive' and 'taking control' of their lives,
perhaps even 'actualizing themselves' in some manner. But by reading
between the lines of their life stories and linking their adult dilemmas to
conflicts that emerged in their early socialization, one could see that,
rather than being moments of freedom and self-expansion, their important
choices were often rather impulsive and desperate attempts to resolve
long-standing issues stemming from a coincidence of social contradictions
and personal conflict. Such processes can be termed ideological for several
reasons:

Privatization: The individuals tend to interpret their dilemmas as personal
rather than public issues. *Example*: A single mother struggling to make
ends meet finds herself choosing between loneliness and poverty, on the
one hand, and the company of less than desirable men who might help
pay for groceries, on the other. Social forces encourage her to blame
herself for her situation, rather than the husband who left her and misses
his child support payments, the company that keeps laying her off, or the
government that has failed to develop policies to provide affordable
housing.

Identification: The solutions to which individuals are impelled often involve drastic measures that cut off life possibilities rather than working towards compromises that might minimize loss and emotional pain. *Example*: A father living in constant turmoil because his job cuts into his time with his young children, and also does not pay him well enough to support them adequately, decides he must take a second job. A kind of self-punishment drives him further from his children and maximizes his productivity in the economic sphere. It is as if an inner authority (actually an external one) says to him, 'If you aren't making it financially, you aren't working hard enough'. This sort of self-castigation is frequently linked to a psychosocial defence mechanism known as *identification with the aggressor*, implying that one agrees with the judgement of the powerful other and metes out the appropriate punishment to oneself.

Insecurity: The individuals' capacities for critical reflection and self-understanding in relation to their dilemmas and choices are constrained by anxiety and fear. *Example*: A very talented man repeatedly withdraws from the fields that interest him just as he is about to achieve recognition for his accomplishments. He accounts for these decisions in terms of a loss of interest, but it is clear from other aspects of his life narrative that he is motivated by a powerful unconscious fear linked to his father's abusive style, which in turn was linked to insecurity about his social status.

Identification with the aggressor and privatization can combine to create an insecure psyche that, in attempts to bolster itself, leans on clichés and common sense to the extent that reflection is impossible and, failing reflection, finds security in closing off dialogue with self and others about basic needs. Action is then guided, not by reflection and intersubjective understanding, but by reactive impulses or 'conditioned reflexes' (Narr 1985). As Adorno might put it, ideology fills the air by day with pseudo-understanding and the appearance of communication to hide the fact that by night it cuts off the tongues of those who would speak. Habermas calls this silencing *delinguistification* and links it to the colonization of the lifeworld in the service of system needs (Habermas 1984). In other words, ideology operates in various ways to subject individuals to processes that produce and reproduce the very social order that hinders their development.

These comments immediately move us on to controversial terrain because a standard refrain these days is that ideology is like culture: 'People will always be subject to ideologies; they can only get rid of one ideology by adopting another'. This argument is based on the inadequate value-neutral definition of ideology. The argument can be stated more carefully from a postmodern perspective, however. For example, critics of the notion of ideology can point out that if ideology refers to a state of not knowing something, it implicitly refers to a state of knowing, that is, to a truth beyond false consciousness. This point, in conjunction with the fact that neo-Marxists who argue for the usefulness of the concept of ideology apparently feel they know something that the subjects of ideology do not, logically leads to the question: How do the former know that the truth they perceive and hope to transmit to the masses is not equally ideological?

This critique, which has usually been presented by conservatives who prefer not to recognize their own stake in maintaining the status quo and is now advanced by advocates of postmodernist positions who rightfully question Utopian and totalizing discourses, must be taken very seriously. Unfortunately, both neo-Marxists and postmodernists have structured the debate between them around an impoverished concept of ideology that rarely takes into account the ways in which the ideological is actually lived by its subjects. The concept of ideology emerged with modernity itself (Eagleton 1991) to designate the discursive opposite of the modern ideal of rational and scientific discourse. It was interpreted in early Marxist circles as a set of intellectual operations serving the interests of those in power. As a result, ideology is seen primarily as one pole of the rationality–irrationality or truth–falsehood continuum. Individuals affected by ideology are viewed as simply having the wrong ideas about their situation and therefore not acting in their own objective interests. The purely cognitive definition of ideology in terms of truth and falsehood leaves one with little sense of why they do not assess their situations more adequately in the first place and why they maintain such incorrect assessments in spite of the states of suffering, deprivation and alienation.

To transcend this gap in understanding, two efforts would be necessary. First, the linkages between institutionalized power and both the form and content of ideology would have to be more carefully specified with an eye to how those linkages are imposed on individuals. Second, the motivational and emotional underpinnings of ideological processes at the level of the individual and concrete institutions would need to be determined. In the second arena, a psychological perspective has more to contribute than to the first, which would require ethnographic and sociological investigations. In the remainder of this section I primarily examine the affective constraints to moving beyond ideology. This will permit me to take into account the postmodernist critique of positions based on views of the subject as capable of autonomous rationality (i.e. non-ideological understandings and actions) while holding out the possibility of achieving a subjective process that is less ideological.

For the moment, I must set aside concerns about the particular content of the ideological processes in question. Doing so is problematic because the function and mechanism of the ideological varies according to context. Furthermore, at high levels of abstraction it becomes more difficult to return to the practical implications of the analysis. Nevertheless, it is worthwhile to examine the general manner in which ideological processes of diverse sorts all manage to capture subjects and drive them to deny their own interests and even act in opposition to them.

To avoid unnecessary confusion I will restate the 'critical' definitions of ideology and intersubjectivity. By ideology, I refer to a system of practices and representations that produce, maintain and reproduce social relations of domination. This is to reject the neutral definition of ideology that equates it with any system of beliefs, attitudes and opinions without regard for their practical functions in multiple contexts. The neutral definition leads directly to the sort of unproductive relativism that permits one to say, as so many do these days, 'You have your ideology, I have mine. How nice!'

The concept of ideology is only useful to the extent that it links cognitive and affective practices at the individual and group levels to the negation of personal and group interests in the service of the irrational requirements of the social order. We will have to leave open the complex question as to how to distinguish real interests from manufactured and manipulated ones. At the psychological level of analysis, we can make plenty of headway even before entering into such matters.

By intersubjectivity, I mean an intrapsychic and interpersonal process of symbolic communication (including 'action') in which participants' interests, desires, dilemmas and doubts are expressed openly in conjunction with a growing comprehension of the functioning of the social order in relation to these interests. In other contexts, intersubjectivity is referred to as critical consciousness, reflexivity, or (in Habermas) communicative competence.

What can a critical psychology tell us about the transformation that occurs in the movement between ideological states and intersubjectivity?

In the context of advanced capitalism, ideology frequently exercises its function *at the level of the individual* through various types of splits between intellectual knowledge, language, perception of social reality and affective experience. In ideology-determined self-understanding and activity, one finds the following 'symptoms' where one might expect fuller experience characterized by feelings appropriate to the subject's thoughts and actions:

- Automatic acts unmediated by reflection
- Blocked communication regarding sensed needs
- Inability to express anger over exploitation
- Resignation to avoidable suffering
- Fragmentation of consciousness

In these and related symptoms, the subject may be vaguely aware that things are not going well and that it might be better to pursue another course of action, but is incapable of dominating what I will call an *ideological formation*. Ideological formations erode possibilities for intersubjectivity and the development of solidarity for effective action. At junctures where domination or oppression might be challenged by direct communication about a state of suffering or an important need, ideological formations incline people to get drunk or otherwise drug themselves, give up before they begin, submit, avoid conflict, accept injustice, ignore their boredom, remain isolated, surrender their freedoms, and so forth. An important dimension of any ideological process is thus the degree of 'splitting' (to borrow loosely from clinical terminology) that subjects must undertake in order to avoid challenging their subjection and exclusion from the spheres of communication in which decisions affecting their lives are made.

Across the social sciences, the liberal concept of the subject as an autonomous and rational entity has been a major obstacle in studies of ideology and has contributed to the marginalization of psychoanalytic insights. According to the liberal notion of the subject, one assumed that, since subjects are autonomous and rational, they must be acting on the basis of what they think; therefore, the problem of ideology was seen as being due to not having correct ideas. This set up the orthodox Marxist notion of ideology as 'false consciousness', a view that emphasizes subjects' allegiance to cognitions (ideas and attitudes) that serve the ruling class. This notion has been rightly criticized for many reasons. From the psychological perspective, it clearly ignores the role of personality structures and styles that routinely sabotage purely educational efforts to help people transcend ideological states. Equally problematic, however, are the structuralist approaches to ideology, typified by Althusser (cf. Eagleton 1991). Althusser conceives of the individual subject as totally subjected, a mere effect of its social positioning. This position denies a priori the possibility of movement towards intersubjectivity and ignores the complexity and at least partial autonomy of the subject. In contrast to the liberal and structuralist views, many postmodern concepts of the subject tend to take the psychoanalytic principle of the divided subject more fully into account and foster an understanding of how it can be that the possession of correct ideas about social reality can coincide with action serving ruling interests or how inadequate conceptions of the social order can sometimes coexist with effective action against domination.

A few examples might help indicate the sort of process involved in ideological formations. Imagine a person walking with a friend who is not paying much attention to the physical environment. The friend says, 'Watch out! You're going to run into a wall'. The other acknowledges the warning but continues on his way. When he hits the wall, he exclaims, 'Hey, I ran into a wall! Why didn't you tell me?' In this case, a sort of disjunction between cognition and real understanding due to an inability to concentrate sets up an action with undesired consequences.

A second analogy introduces another dimension to the equation, a dimension that helps to differentiate the ideological process from ordinary neurosis. Two lovers find themselves losing their initial mutual infatuation. Usually one of them arrives earlier at this point and begins to question the relationship, to be bored, to criticize the other, and so forth. Nevertheless, they both continue as before, hoping that the infatuation will spring back to life or that something will happen to make the problem go away. The parallel with ideological processes can be found in the split between the awareness that something is seriously wrong, the behaviour that denies this and the course of erotic desire, which seems to follow its own rules. In the romantic scenario, the desire of one of the lovers puts herself or himself down and lifts the other to an idealized status, all the while denying what is seen but not 'processed', that is, the fact that the other is neither ideal nor all that interested in the former.

In an ideological formation, in contrast to the neurotic relationship, the other (whether it be the state, the company, the boss or the master) also functions in one way or another from an idealized position. The worker, for example, knows very well that the boss is far from being his friend or ally, but the ideological impulse urges him to accept the boss's excuses when he explains, seated in his new Mercedes Benz, that this year profits were again too low to justify raises for the workers. Worse yet, the worker almost agrees when management blames him and his co-workers for the consequences of management's poor planning.

The ideological role of the splits between awareness, behaviour and desire can be further illustrated through reference to the situation of the middle classes in advanced industrial societies. Most citizens in these societies are familiar with the fact that, for global ecological reasons, they cannot continue consuming manufactured products at the levels to which they are accustomed. They are also quite aware of the sacrifices in quality of life that they make by dedicating their energies to earning the money necessary to maintain these levels of consumption. Nevertheless, the vast majority continues working too much or too hard in order to maintain and increase their material standard of living and to purchase each new 'essential' product that enters the market.

Apart from the attendant ecological problems, perhaps this scene would not be especially problematic; one could simply interpret it as the effect of a culture that chooses to place value primarily on material possessions. But recent developments show that the system is also internally contradictory. The typical family currently devotes 10 per cent or more of its income towards interest on previous consumer purchases (not including mortgage interest), and manages to do this despite the fact that the real purchasing power of the typical family has declined over the last decade, a fact masked by the increasing numbers of women who have entered the work-force to make ends meet in the family budget. In this situation, to continue buying is not a rational act, not in one's objective interest. The decision to work more to earn more money is reasonable, but the added income does not always improve the situation due to added material and emotional costs (need for a second car, less time with children, physical exhaustion, nervous strain, etc.).

What is going on here? It would be difficult to explain this scene without recourse to the concept of ideology. In this case, the concept allows one to take into account simultaneously the fact that the actors at some level know that what they are doing is not in their objective interest and the fact that they keep doing it anyway. They continue because their self-evaluations and social identities are so heavily determined by symbols associated with buying, even when this motive is masked by the idea of providing well for the family. Furthermore, the ritual of consumption depends less on the nature of the product itself than on the emotional gratification of sensing one's power to buy it and to be the sort of person who possesses it. It is as if consumers fear they will die if they cannot purchase that new video-camera. What completes the ideological chain here is that this fear fuels the economy of corporate capitalism. This particular form of psychological slavery is but one of the ideological formations associated with the colonization of the lifeworld under capitalist modernization. Side by side with consumerism, one finds the usual racism and sexism dividing workers, tolerance of authoritarian management practices, and a variety of relatively recent privatized or individualized ways of organizing the self in relation to socio-political domination (Gregg 1991).

BEYOND IDEOLOGY

Thus far we have considered the ideological process at the level of the individual in terms of its form and social function. Now I take up the thorny issue of movement beyond the ideological. Following Martín-Baró (1994), I will refer to this as *de-ideologization*. Given ideology's status as a certain privatization of communication or as a blockage of symbolic process, it would be logical to look for de-ideologization in a process of resymbolization of experience and resocialization of communication. Such processes, which of course occur in manifold patterns, can be examined in terms of various key moments, in particular those which involve a reorganization of subjects' stances towards their strivings for a different order of things.

De-ideologization can begin with the awareness of a kernel of desire that seeks expression, a partially suppressed affectively charged image of a more satisfying type of social relationship or personal project. One must note that, while the desire fuelling this moment may be for egalitarian or caring relations between humans, initial images of an alternative order are themselves mediated by the ideological process. They may incorporate a symbolic reaction to oppression and domination. The slave, for example, imagines a time when he will have his own slaves. The factory worker craves the extravagant sports car driven by the executive. Nevertheless, this moment is significant because desire that has previously been bound up by fear and anxiety breaks loose and initiates the subject's imaginative movement towards an alternative order. For this to happen, a preliminary identification with the aggressor may be necessary. To move beyond the safer, compromised situation, a certain injection of 'courage' is required. This often seems to stem from a combination of indignation and the idea of exercising power over others. Even when an individual enjoys group solidarity in a manner that prefigures wider egalitarian social relations, the psyche tends to trail behind, since it is essentially an ideological structure. At first, the psyche is structurally capable only of imagining and identifying with a role reversal. It would rather be on top than on the bottom. As a consequence of this, the psychological moment in question is generally a reactive one provoked by a particularly aggravating external act of oppression. It is unlikely that the necessary structural switch could occur without such provocation, except perhaps in wishful daydreaming.

This is not to deny the possibility of a subjective attitude less determined by unequal relations of power – a longing for equality, just treatment, respect and full participation. But what would be the source and the nature of such a desire? Finding an answer is complicated by the fact that the concept of desire is a slippery one. The beginnings of an answer regarding the desire for egalitarian relations can be found in the recent work of North American feminist psychoanalysts, in particular that of Jessica Benjamin. Benjamin (1977) develops a critique of Theodor Adorno's idea that the psychological source of the revolutionary impulse could be nothing other than a reaction to the internalized authority of the patriarchal father. Benjamin correctly perceived in this a strategical dead end. If personal motivations towards the establishment of a just society depended on the preservation of the father's arbitrary power in the process of socialization, institutional conditions for the development of non-authoritarian personalities and the practice of egalitarian relations could never exist.

Benjamin thus sought another model in which hope for social change might be based and found it in non-authoritarian parent–child relations of mutual recognition, play and imitation (Benjamin 1988). This makes sense. Only powerful memories of more enjoyable experiences than those associated with subjection could motivate movement towards egalitarian rather than domineering social relations. The matter is complicated, however, by the fact that childhood forms of egalitarian interaction depend largely on mirroring and imitation. While these forms escape vertical power schemes, the subject can remain trapped by a horizontal fusion of representations of self and other. Psychological separation and individuation, of course, begin on the basis of this sort of fusion, but de-ideologization depends on a transcendence of primitive fusion, mimesis and symbiosis. In this sense, de-ideologization is partly comparable to the transitions to higher stages of moral development proposed by Kohlberg (cf. Habermas 1990). Both self and others must be recognized as independent subjects rather than 'used' as extensions or interpreted as projections of self. Thus, we may conclude that de-ideologization will involve a simultaneous de-idealization of self and others along the vertical dimension of power and differentiation of self from other on the horizontal dimension of attachment.

THE ENSUING STRUGGLE

We can conceptualize the first stage of de-ideologization as the beginnings of an emancipatory symbol structured and stimulated by identification with the aggressor, sadistic impulses, and idealized and fused representations of self and other. The difficulty of development beyond this stage becomes apparent as we examine a step further along the road.

Subjects who have begun to move towards de-ideologization – that is, towards a coherence of perception, thought, affect and action in light of newly recognized interests – enter a phase of psychosocial crisis in whatever spheres of life are being called into question. On one hand, they experience new hope and sense the possibility of life in a different world. On the other hand, they have a painful awareness of their past suffering and begin to realize the risks they run by pushing for change. They may experience a powerful combination of fear and anxiety: fear of the reactions of the powers that be, and anxiety stemming from the difficult and uncontrollable processes of identity change. Furthermore, they run the risk of losing their usual sources of social support as well as whatever 'secondary gains' they might have earned previously by not challenging power structures (being the boss's favourite, stability of employment, etc.).

The Yugoslav philosopher Zizek provides a useful example of the difficulty of de-ideologization in *The Sublime Object of Ideology* (1989). In particular, he highlights the subject's own role in maintaining his or her subjection to domination. (This is not a popular stance since it is difficult to differentiate it from 'blaming the victim', but when one remembers that subjective structures are, in the final analysis, reflections of social relations, this issue falls by the wayside.) Drawing on Hegel and Lacan, Zizek analyses the situation of the fragile victim who passively observes and suffers the evils of the world, believing herself to be innocent of any participation in the creation of that world. This sort of subject

> structures the 'objective' social world in advance so that it is able to assume, to play in it the role of the fragile, innocent and passive victim. This, then, is Hegel's fundamental lesson: when we are active, when we intervene in the world through a particular act, the real act is not this particular, empirical, factual intervention (or non-intervention); the real act is of a strictly symbolic nature, it consists in the very mode in which we structure the world, our perception of it, in advance, in order to make our intervention possible, in order to open in it the space for our activity (or inactivity).
>
> (Zizek 1989: 215–216)

To illustrate this point, Zizek describes the suffering mother in patriarchal society, exploited by all the members of her family, who does all the domestic work, and despite the fact that she continually complains about her oppressed situation, finds her identity only in this self-sacrificing role. The mother's complaint is also a demand that others continue to exploit her in order to give her life meaning. Zizek continues:

> [T]he true meaning of the mother's complaint is: 'I'm ready to give up, to sacrifice everything... *everything but the sacrifice itself!*' What the poor mother must do, if she really wants to liberate herself from this domestic enslavement, is to *sacrifice the sacrifice itself* – to stop accepting or even actively sustaining the social network (of the family) which confers on her the role of exploited victim.
>
> (Zizek 1989: 216)

In this example we glimpse the fundamental *form* of the ideological: '[T]he subject overlooks his or her *formal responsibility* for the given state of things' by being identified imaginatively with the *content* of the subjected position, in this case, the beauty of self-sacrifice (ibid.: 217). Such predetermination of the symbolic space to be filled by one's activity accounts for the difficulty of liberating oneself from the subjected identities that organize, from the psychological point of view, self-destructive and self-denying behaviour.

In conjunction with such realizations, it is common to hear debates over the relative primacy of action over thought in social and personal change. One camp claims that change is largely a matter of changing objective behaviour, in the hope that through practice subjects will learn and adapt their thinking to their new experiences. The other camp argues that there is something false, which certainly will not serve us well in the long run, in actions that are not accompanied by changes in emotional character and deep subjective comprehension of the necessary change. In the first position one senses the impatience of youth; in the second the paralyzing pessimism or scepticism that stems from the experience of failure in poorly-planned action projects. In this regard perhaps it is sufficient to recall Gramsci's maxim: Pessimism of the intellect, optimism of the will. But I would also argue that this false dichotomy of thought versus action can be transcended in practice only if we take seriously enough the obstacles in both realms, rather than downplaying the importance of either.

Without doubt, the outcome of the second moment of de-ideologization usually depends primarily on the role played by others involved in the person's life, be they friends, family, union or party members. It seems that a certain identification with the strength of the group is essential to confront the objective fears and subjective anxieties generated by the first movements towards intersubjectivity. In the lives of the persons I have studied in some depth, this stage of uncertainty, of gains and losses, or self-reorganization, attempts and failures, may persist for years before the person settles back into the previous ideological state or establishes a new order in a particular sphere of life (Sloan 1987). In this regard I agree with the psychoanalytic position which holds that rushing or forcing change at the personal level is hardly worth the trouble, for if it is not accompanied by significant self-understanding, subsequent failures will merely reinforce timidity in the face of future opportunities. This does not imply that a friend, a therapist, a spouse or a work group should not convey to the person clear visions of alternative forms of action and understanding, but rather that one must keep in mind the idiosyncratic (but socially produced) difficulty of certain changes for given individuals. I wonder, for example, how many activists have lost valuable potential partners because in their frustration with the slowness of such change processes, they end up shouting in the faces of the slow to comprehend, somehow imagining that they will be heard.

In this second moment of de-ideologization, then, spaces open up for new identifications and associated practical roles. A struggle of images takes place, the outcome of which will affect the degree of movement the subject can make. Usually the positions available for new identifications are represented concretely by relatives, friends, media personalities or historical figures, yet the process remains nevertheless heavily mediated by the psychological sequelae of the individual's life experiences. Knowing sociological characteristics of the individual is not enough to predict either the process or the outcome of movements towards subjectivity. Despite this fact, the motivation to carry through with a process of transformation can grow or diminish in relation to concrete possibilities for thinking and acting in ways related to the new forms of identification that are available. For this reason, every formal and informal institution that plays a role in socialization and affects us daily must be examined with regard to the types of communication and activity it fosters for its participants. If subjects encounter spaces favourable to the articulation of their needs and their desires for change, they can more easily transcend fears and anxieties associated with leaving subjected identities behind.

Movements towards intersubjectivity are processes and not final destinations. In connection with this insight, a third moment of de-ideologization can be isolated. It comes after the consolidation and integration of new forms of interaction. Many of us have probably seen how the achievements of de-ideologization gradually lose their freshness and are converted into habits of thought and action almost as automatic as those that they replaced. It is in part because this happens that postmodern critics of the notion of ideology can argue that one ideological discourse merely replaces another. On the surface it does appear that this is the case. But the fact remains that the new habitual thoughts and actions that were established through a process of de-ideologization are by definition more 'in touch' with social reality and the subject's interests. For example, 'habitual' recourse to democratic processes of conflict resolution must be understood as preferable to prior meek submissiveness or autocracy. Even those who argue for radical relativism continue to harbour personal preferences for certain types of experiences, relationships and societies. To ground adequately a project of social transformation, we must insist on the possibility of meaningful improvements at the individual, group and societal levels as well as the possibility of collectively determining what these improvements should be and how to implement them.

It is important to acknowledge, however, that many neo-Marxist conceptions of ideology at least implicitly refer to a Utopian de-ideologized condition. In view of the postmodern critique, it would be better to think in terms of partial de-ideologizing movements on the basis of which forms of interaction and institutions can open new spaces for the realization of individual and collective yearnings.

The two camps in the debate have often failed to understand each other because they normally analyse the ideational *contents* of ideology abstracted from socio-historical contexts. Only when these are seen in relation to the general form and quality of communication pertaining to action in a particular sphere of social relations can the extent of de-ideologization be determined. De-ideologization should thus not be viewed as a total change from falsehood to truth. It is instead a process by which previously privatized thought and desire are resymbolized and resocialized in communicative action.

Chapter 7

The destruction of meaning

The damaged lives we live in the context of modernity can, to a large extent, be traced to the operations of ideological formations set up by the colonization of the lifeworld. Armed with a critical concept of ideology, we can now examine how the disruption of the symbolic processes of the lifeworld produces the psychopathologies of modern times. Here we will finally begin to understand the process through which modernity destroys the psychosocial foundations for the subjective sense of meaningfulness.

SYMBOLIC PROCESSES AND MEANING

First, a brief commentary on the nature of symbols is in order. Meaning depends on the interplay of symbols. One way of understanding symbols is to see them as effects produced by relations between signifiers (e.g. a flag, a cross) and signifieds (e.g. patriotism, Christianity). Since the realm of that which is signified is always heterogeneous, signifiers shift and slide in relation to each other as they are used in communication referring to the signified. As a result, symbols constantly undergo processes of decoding and recoding. Meanings are thus always 'under construction'.

Meanings related to personal identity are regularly reworked in the same fashion (Jackson 1984; Wiersma 1988). Identity or self could be construed as a process of positioning a signifier (the 'I') in relation to a field of signifieds ('me'). Symbols of self (I–me structures, images of self in relation to others) contribute to the construction of meaning by positioning core conscious self-images (i.e. 'consciousness') in relation to the flow of experience. Memories of the past, awareness of the present and anticipated futures make available multiple aspects of self for use as meanings are constructed in an ongoing fashion: feelings, intentions, hopes, the sensed expectations and desires of particular others, and a more generalized social world.

This view of symbols as they relate to personal identity suggests the idea that a connection between rich textures of self-images to broad, deep and long experience in the world of others would make possible a sense of meaningfulness in living. To illustrate this, consider a few examples of moments that are often mentioned as providing a special sense of meaningfulness: the birth of a child (could be a symbol of the extension of oneself, union with the other parent, continuity across generations); completion of a difficult task (could symbolize self-expression, the fruit of joint efforts, a step towards a long-term goal); producing a work of art (could symbolize almost anything – human creativity, resolution of conflict or tension, expression of a truth). One may note that each of these experiences of meaning shares multiple referents that link self to world in ways that matter because they communicate. Symbols accumulate power by encompassing multiple layers of referents and the most powerful symbols seem to lend themselves to multiple levels of interpretation.

Following a basic psychoanalytic assumption, the role of desire in the symbolic determination of meaning must be emphasized. Desire is especially salient in the symbolic processes of early childhood. As Chapter 4 indicates, the early socialization of the child involves a dialectical interaction between the child's organismic needs and their satisfaction by caretakers in a given socio-cultural context. Specific interaction paradigms are internalized as a consequence of characteristic actions on the part of caretakers and temperamentally determined responses on the child's part. These are sedimented in affectively toned representations of self-in-relation-to-others, which operate as if they were forms imposed upon the body, providing frameworks for muscular action, emotional expression and interpersonal understanding. It is indeed language, in the broad sense of the term, that begins to dominate the child's experience of its body. Needs are defined and expressed in terms of collectively understood concepts, words, gestures and signs. Language skills develop specifically in order to facilitate interaction, interpersonal negotiation, and the satisfaction of needs.

Consider this example of an interaction between a 3-year-old girl and her father, who is caught up in a conversation with the girl's mother:

Daddy!
Huh?
Daddy!
Yes?
Wanna play trucks with me?
Not now. Daddy is tired. Play by yourself for a while and then we'll make some cookies together. OK?
OK! Can we make chocolate chip cookies?
Sure.

The child wants to play, to interact with someone. The particular form of interaction is not especially important to her. Her fundamental need is to feel that she is a part of the father's world and that he is a part of hers. The father offers a substitute hope that will probably satisfy his daughter temporarily. The *symbol* of togetherness provided by the possibility of making cookies together fills the immediate emotional need of the child. And so it goes. The felt needs of the child are by necessity repeatedly deferred. Layers and layers of feeling-laden symbols of interaction and gratification fill the memory and provide a basis for conscious images of self in relation to others. Gradually, the corporeal–emotional needs of the child are displaced into forms of play, fantasy and requests for substitute gratification of more primary urges for closeness, comfort, recognition and reassurance. Symbols, such as 'daddy and me making cookies', thus derive part of their meaning through a connection with the movement of desire in an interpersonal context in connection with an internalized interaction pattern.

Several aspects are essential to this relation: triangulation (self–desire–object), communication, recognition and understanding. A term that comes to mind in attempting to describe the quality of symbolic experience is Dilthey's (1961) 'lived experience'. It conveys a wholeness or fullness that is not present when meaning is absent or weak. This fullness stems from a relatively unconstrained interplay of memory (e.g. the girl's pleasant recollection of the last time she and her father made cookies), desire (bodily pleasure in eating, search for recognition and closeness) and communication (her ability to represent her desire in speech and to feel that her need has been understood). In summary, *symbolization* involves a linguistic–cultural mediation of the relation between subject and object. It builds on the basic processes of perception, sensation and memory to create a meaningful social interaction in which desire is expressed.

Let us imagine that the father, for neurotic reasons, had experienced his daughter's request for attention as intolerable. Perhaps he ignored her, yelled at her, or even hit her. If this were to occur repeatedly, the girl's experience of her need for attention would eventually be linked to unconscious, negatively toned representations of her father's neglect or anger. The girl's subsequent attempts (even much later in life) to express legitimate needs for help or company would pass through this filter before being communicated, perhaps shaping her style of making requests such that her requests would not be taken seriously – for example, by inducing her to act as if she does not really want what she is asking for, does not deserve attention, or expect her wish to be granted. This filter would exercise this constraining force because the girl would be unable to differentiate between her image of herself with a legitimate need and the image of the uncaring or punishing father. Desiring self and 'mean daddy' would be fused in a combination of negative affects, including the girl's pain at being neglected, rejected, or struck, and her own hostile reaction to such treatment, which she could not easily communicate for fear of being further rejected. The establishment of this sort of negatively toned, undifferentiated set of images of self-in-relation-to-others breaks down the fullness of symbolic experience in a particular sphere of a person's life. In place of communication, there is silence or ineffective action; in place of comprehension, there is constraint. The wishes and hopes of childhood become vague and private lifelong yearnings.

DESYMBOLIZATION

This view of the formation of privatized thoughts and silenced desires parallels that of Alfred Lorenzer (1976), the German psychoanalyst to whom Habermas turned for a linguistic reading of psychoanalytic theory (cf. Habermas 1971; Bleicher 1980). Lorenzer's work provides clues as to how to understand ideology in terms of *desymbolization*. Lorenzer describes the process of desymbolization in Freudian terms as a splitting of affect from thought, but, in contrast to Freud, who uses hydraulic metaphors to account for repression and other defensive activity, Lorenzer focuses on linguistic–symbolic aspects of defence.

When communication and action are not subjected to constraints or coercion linked to the effects of domination in social relations, they are characterized by a coherence of thought and feeling. Simply put, what is said and done is intended and felt. The capacity to maintain this level of integration can be understood in terms of object relations theory (cf. Chapter 4). Such capacity is grounded in fairly advanced development of personality structure including tolerance of ambivalent and de-idealized images of self and other as well as differentiation of self from other. Personal experience associated with such coherence of thought, affect and action may be referred to as symbolized experience.

Defensive processes occur when the affects called forth by interpersonal conflict, abuse or other trauma cannot be managed without a regression to a less integrated organization of the psyche. Lorenzer portrays this as a breakdown of symbolization into *signs* (affectless, objectifying thought) and *stereotypes* (split-off affect and impulse). Signs can be constituted by rationalization, intellectualization, denial or any cognitive procedure that avoids linking an unacceptable idea or intention to the affect that might have been associated with it were it not for anxiety, guilt or fear.

I suggest that stereotypes (which are not to be confused with the social psychological use of the term) can be understood in object relational terms as negatively-toned affect associated with fused images of self and other. Stereotypes constitute what psychoanalytic theory describes as unconscious intentions. They find expression in action when aspects of an interpersonal situation or *scene* resonate with elements of the initial relationship in which desymbolization became necessary. As mentioned above, this *acting out* is likely to be accompanied by cognitive moves at the sign level to excuse or justify the impulsive action.

To illustrate the action of stereotypes, imagine how, as an adult, the rejected or neglected girl described earlier might behave when she encounters a cool and distant, but physically attractive man. Especially if the man communicates ambivalence about getting involved with her, or if she can interpret him as being unavailable because he is already involved with another, she is likely to find him even more attractive, to behave in a clingy fashion and to find herself rejected anew. In short, she recognizes or constructs an emotionally charged *scene* in which she clearly recognizes her role. In a version of the 'repetition compulsion' described by Freud, the present scene evokes impulsive or compulsive action connected to the stereotype around which unresolved anger and idealization of her father are constellated. *Post hoc*, she might rationalize the negative outcome in language that actually describes her father: 'He was more interested in someone else [mother]'.

As this example indicates, action informed by stereotypes is problematic for several reasons. First, it is not free (although it may be experienced by the actor as liberating). It is compulsive, automatic, driven. Second, stereotyped action bypasses or cuts short self-reflection and interpersonal communication in which other action possibilities could be considered. Third, such action tends not to be in one's best interest, although it may in some sense be effective (due to its dramatic character, its impact, the attention it draws, etc.).

These three characteristics are shared with ideology. Lorenzer's objective in laying out this framework for the understanding of repression is to show that desymbolization is part and parcel of any ideological process. Furthermore, the neuroticizing interaction paradigms one internalizes in childhood socialization are generally not private family matters, but extensions of social contradictions (such as class or gender inequality) into the structuring of the psyche.

In the analysis of capitalist modernization, it is tempting to draw a parallel between the predominance of cognitive–instrumental rationality and the socio-cultural reinforcement of desymbolization. In contexts where objectifying attitudes towards the self (and self-practices as well) are rewarded with status, power and money, desymbolization rather than integration is being fostered. Success in the system follows the one who is cool, unemotional, focused on tasks, willing to suppress objections and facile in 'appropriate' self-presentation and impression management. The degree of self-control necessary to maintain such states can only be accomplished by a great degree of emotional management. Of course, while profitability and productivity may be sustained at the system level, a price is paid sooner or later by the individual who adopts this narcissistic style in psychosomatic illness, addictions, ruined relationships, midlife crises and subjective emptiness. Mental illness becomes the last container for the inhumane sequelae of capitalist social relations.

THE NARCISSISM-DEPRESSION CONTINUUM

At this point, we can delve further into the symptomatology of two common modern psychic disorders. In psychoanalytic circles, it has long been assumed that healthy identity formation depends on the resolution of emotional contradictions through internalization and identification processes of the sort associated with the Oedipal crisis in the nuclear family. In particular, capacities for full symbolic thought, relatedness and emotional maturity depend on a relatively successful resolution of Oedipal issues.

To these considerations we may now add the common observation by psychoanalysts regarding the nature of the disorders they find themselves treating in advanced industrial societies (Jones 1981; Frosh 1989; Lasch 1979; Kernberg 1975). It appears that over the last fifty years or so, they have observed the decline of the classical, Oedipally constellated neuroses such as phobias and hysterical and obsessional disorders. Instead their patients can be described clinically as belonging to the realm of the personality disorders, the narcissistic, the depressive, the sadomasochistic, the antisocial and the borderline, for example. Each of these disorders is characterized by a failure to achieve or maintain the higher level symbolic processes that support the capacity for both autonomous thought, impulse control and intersubjective communication. They are also regarded as stemming from failure to resolve pre-Oedipal as well as Oedipal issues. The personality disorders are thus typified by lack of differentiation of self from other, incapacity for autonomous self-reflection, severe problems with intimacy, impulsive or self-destructive behaviour and difficulty finding satisfaction in one's pursuits.

In this regard, consider the way the psychoanalyst Kernberg describes a particular group of modern patients:

> There are patients who describe a painful and disturbing subjective experience which they frequently refer to as a feeling of emptiness. In typical cases, it is as if this emptiness were their basic modality of subjective experience from which they attempt to escape by engagement in many activities or in frantic social interactions, by the ingestion of drugs or alcohol, or by attempts to obtain instinctual gratifications through sex, aggression, food, or compulsive activities that reduce their focusing on their inner experience.
>
> (Kernberg 1985: 213–214)

Kernberg goes on to describe a contrasting group of patients who surrender to the sense of emptiness and lead robotic, dull lives. Aren't these descriptions of the damaged goods produced by the social relations of advanced capitalism?

Let's continue by taking a look at those whose upbringing prepares them poorly for standard forms of success, whether it be because they are too empathic, fragile, sensitive or otherwise incapable of sustaining the idealized self-images and identifications with power required to impose their own agendas on others. Judging from the soaring sales of antidepressants, depression is probably the most common outcome of socialization in the advanced sectors of corporate capitalism. Although they actually represent more coherent personality structures, depressive styles have been interpreted as 'failed' narcissistic styles (Miller 1986). In depressives we see the collapse of the grandiose self-image that protects narcissists from their own rage at not getting basic emotional needs met. Depressives thus regulate their affect by other means: inaction, passivity, sleep, loss of appetite or overeating, melancholy, longing for intimacy, abandonment of personal projects, or unwillingness to hope. In a sense, depressives are too deeply related to, as opposed to just manipulating, the world of others; they have only withdrawn because others have been disappointing. More than narcissists, they struggle against the sensation of an internal 'black hole' (Grotstein 1991). As a consequence, positively toned identifications that fuel realistic self-esteem are strained, unresolved negatively toned representations of self and other colour one's outlook, and depression takes hold. The culture suggests various solutions, some of which involve reattachments to objects, such as falling in love, getting a new job, taking a vacation in an exotic place, or buying a new car. It appears that a new style, equally problematic, may be developing to challenge such solutions. In a recently noted alternative to depression and narcissism labelled anti-narcissism, individuals apparently cultivate a negative narcissism, refusing to nurture themselves or to make use of talents, as a way of remaining angrily dependent (Bollas 1989).

How do narcissists and depressives differ in relation to desymbolization? I would argue that both lean experientially towards the drained plane of signs to defend against engulfment by rage. Narcissists, however, attend to the fragile pole of the self, monitoring their value and acting in ways that sustain required self-images. Perhaps because they cannot maintain idealized self-images, depressives seem to focus consciously more on the object pole, that is, on the importance of the other (and the negative aspects of self in relation to the other). Their clinging to an idealized object as well as their melancholy moods and emotional numbness are usually interpreted as defences against their anger at abandonment, at the failure of the world to provide that to which they feel entitled. Both narcissists and depressives are likely to succumb to stereotyped acting out when their basic defensive process is threatened. The psychoanalytic clinical literature would suggest that, when this happens, narcissists are inclined towards sadistic behaviour, while depressives take it out on themselves masochistically (cf. Miller 1986; Gear *et al.* 1981).

It is difficult, even in case studies, to pinpoint the origins of these personality styles in early childhood. As Earnest (1992) suggests, however, what ends up mattering in ideology criticism is the fact that when social relations are characterized by domination, exploitation and injustice, communication is systematically distorted in processes of desymbolization that rely on whatever defensive styles are available to the subjects involved. Narcissistic and depressive styles are used here to illustrate two familiar modes of experience that can be linked to the culture and social institutions associated with capitalist modernization. To the extent that they can also be associated with socialization under capitalist imperatives, the two styles reveal the psychic depths to which social contradictions of the economic order may penetrate.

DETERRITORIALIZATION

To launch the final phase of this inquiry, I have chosen to introduce an odd counterpart to Habermas's model, from which we can extract a unique and radical perspective on capitalist modernization and its impact on symbolic processes.

The perspective proposed by the French social theorists Gilles Deleuze and Felix Guattari forces one to turn the coin over to inspect modernization from another angle. Their outlook suggests that we inquire whether desymbolization might in fact be a source of energy for revolutionary action, a way of moving beyond the constraining ideological order of a particular culture. Doesn't the colonization of the lifeworld at least free us from the fetters of tradition and set up new identities for subjects to adopt? Given the fact that resymbolization, such as that which occurs in psychotherapy, has no necessary connection to larger social institutions, isn't it merely a mode of adjustment or adaptation to the status quo, a sort of 'coming to terms' or self-subjection with the social order?

To understand Deleuze and Guattari's vision, let us consider first the fact that all societies, in one way or another, subject their members to a cultural system that organizes, encodes or channels their psychobiological energies, urges and impulses. To put this in Foucault's (1977) terms, the body is disciplined. In this process, everything from table manners to gender identities, from fighting methods to love-making styles, is transmitted in such a way that one usually knows how and what to do in most situations. Furthermore, to the degree that socialization is effective, one eventually even *wants* to do all these things in the prescribed fashion.

To a great extent, this 'enculturation' process is identical with ideologization, the establishment of new subjects within ideological frameworks.

The operation of social power binds and guides the body through systems of practices and representations. The boundary between enculturation and ideologization is a fuzzy one. One must wonder, where does necessary socialization end and unjustifiable domination begin?

In *Anti-Oedipus*, Deleuze and Guattari (1983) analyse social orders in terms of how they encode or *territorialize* energies in some spheres of life, while decoding or *deterritorializing* energies in others (cf. D'Amico 1978; Bogue 1989; Best and Kellner 1991). Here, 'energies' refers to immense 'flows' of intertwined material goods, bodily needs and psychic desires. Coding can be seen as a sort of channeling that occurs through the establishment of routine practices and systems of representation that sustain them. Decoding occurs when these channels break down because existing codes lose their legitimacy due to a failure of authority or because stronger codes replace them.

In Deleuze and Guattari's scheme, two eras preceded capitalism: the 'primitive territorial' order, organized around kinship, and the 'barbarian despotic' order, imposed on the primitive community by the rise of the State and the tyrant who rules it. The despotic State attempts to subject all flows to its control. As a means to this end, numerous inventions (operating at the level of signs) are elaborated: writing, money, taxes, timekeeping, laws and courts. Eventually the despotic system explodes from internal contradictions arising from its efforts to encode and control all flows of goods and desires within it. Capitalism emerges as the socio-political form that transcends this overencoding. Summarizing Deleuze and Guattari on the matter, Bogue writes:

> The tendency of capitalism is to substitute for fixed and limiting relations between men and things an abstract unit of equivalence that allows free exchange and the aleatory substitution, of everything for everything. Not only are equivalences established between goods in an open market, but bodies, actions, ideas, knowledge, fantasies, images function as commodities which can be translated into other commodities.
>
> (Bogue 1989: 100)

The move beyond use value to abstract exchange value in the economic sphere liberates energies bound in precapitalist society and fuels a brush-fire of socio-political and psychocultural shifts (D'Amico 1978). For exchange value to dominate in this manner, everything from wheat to persons must be representable by the same sign (money) and becomes essentially identical. The initial liberation and levelling is, however, followed by a reorganization of economy and psyche by modern policing, administrative control and self-management.

In its 'cynical' desacralization of the modern world, capitalism dissolves all premodern forms of alliances and filiations, shatters all restrictions to economic development, and thereby radically extends the decoding process. . . . Capitalism extends market relations everywhere and creates a growing division of labor, producing the individual with an ego/superego, as well as social and psychic fragmentation.

(Best and Kellner 1991: 89)

The crux of the argument developed by Deleuze and Guattari in *Anti-Oedipus* is that the Oedipal complex, rather than being merely the sign of family-produced neuroses, functions as a defence against the levelling of symbolic life and a dam against desire liberated by capitalist commodity exchange relations. This process is described as a decoding that unhinged social authority from the figures of God, the King and the Father and replaced it with abstract Reason, which itself collapses with the passing of the age of Enlightenment. Previously dominant norms, codes and associated identities and desires broke up in this process and the Oedipal family rose along pre-existing patriarchal lines to contain the chaos. Bogue explains:

Capitalism tends to reduce all social relations to commodity relations of universal equivalency. In this process, it 'deterritorializes' desire by subverting traditional codes that limit and control social relations and production, such as kinship systems, class structures, religious beliefs, folk traditions, customs, and so on. Yet it also simultaneously reterritorializes desire by channeling all production into the narrow confines of the equivalence-form. The Oedipus complex ensures that human desire is concentrated in the nuclear family, and hence individualized, and that only a residual and 'commodified' desire invests the larger social domain, which is regulated by the economic relations of capital.

(Bogue 1989: 88)

The reference here to the production of the individual psyche is important. As despotic power declines, individuals become their own despots. The bourgeois form of the Oedipus complex arises as a reterritorialization of desire freed by the capitalist machine. When the resolution of the Oedipus complex is unsatisfactory, psychoanalytic therapy comes to the rescue. Here we seem to encounter the colonization of the lifeworld described in other terms:

Capitalism subverts all traditional codes, values, and structures that fetter production, exchange, and desire. But it simultaneously 'recodes' everything within the abstract logic of equivalence (exchange-value), 'reterritorializing' them within the state, family, law, commodity logic, banking systems, consumerism, psychoanalysis, and other normalizing institutions. . . . Capitalism re-channels desire and needs into inhibiting psychic and social spaces that control them far more effectively than savage and despotic societies.

(Best and Kellner 1991: 89)

A loose equation can thus be drawn between deterritorialization and the rationalization of the lifeworld (critiques of superstition and Church power, challenging arbitrary parental values, establishing new spaces for dialogue and action). A similar parallel can be drawn between reterritorialization and the colonization of the lifeworld (subjection to the performance principle, social management of the nuclear family, shaping lifestyle choices through advertising). This distinction only holds up momentarily for social or psychological movements that emerge as deterritorialization are simultaneously caught up by reterritorializing forces. For example, the energies liberated by the decline of paternal authority in the bourgeois era were recoded in a 'paranoid' regression to despotic social forms by the rise of Fascism (Bogue 1989). For a more recent example, consider how the energies of punk rock music were quickly commodified and reterritorialized as 'new wave'.

In order to subvert Fascism and commodification at both the social and the individual level, Deleuze and Guattari recommend what they call a 'schizophrenic' process. They are well aware of the sufferings of schizophrenics, but they see in the schizophrenic psyche a form of revolutionary resistance to the capitalist reterritorialization of liberated desire.

[T]he paradigm of the revolutionary is not the disciplined party man, but the schizo-subject, the one who resists the capitalist axiomatic, rejects Oedipus, unscrambles the social codes, and break through the walls of reterritorialization into the realm of flows, intensities, and becoming, thereby threatening the whole capitalist order.

(Best and Kellner 1991: 91–92)

Without getting into the intriguing question of how such psychic states might effectively disrupt the economic order, one can draw from this perspective a clue as to the nature of de-ideologization and resymbolization. Both are moves that de-objectify, de-reify, restoring exactly the sort of temporal and semiotic fluidity that basic psychoanalytic interrogation is supposed to produce (cf. Barratt 1984, 1988, 1993). This can also be understood in Adorno's terms as 'negative dialectical' process (Adorno 1973; Jay 1984; Jameson 1990).

Whether the goal of resymbolization should be sublimation or desublimation, intersubjectivity or schizo-subjectivity, is hotly debated (Frosh 1989). On this issue, the common ground between modernists such as Habermas and postmodernists such as Deleuze and Guattari is their critique of the colonization of the lifeworld employed in the service of market expansion, social administration and socialization. Both positions indicate the need for creating more social and psychological space for the play of desire, complexity of feeling, sensitivity to aesthetic values and individual self-definition. Unfortunately, each of these realms that might find expression in a process of decolonization can also be informed by the operation of stereotypes (which might be viewed by Deleuze–Guattari as clusters of desire split off during encoding processes). In other words, artistic activity could be either the product of stereotyped acting out or the undoing of stereotypes (or both). Political resistance to the colonization of the lifeworld could be merely compulsive or masochistic, or an essential de-ideologizing activity that actually produces desirable change (or both). The question, in short, is: To sublimate or not to sublimate?

SHIFTING FORMS OF DOMINATION

Whether the reader will choose to understand ideological formations in terms of desymbolization or reterritorialization, I cannot predict. In either case, however, one begins to be positioned to interpret the crisis of the modern psyche as a disruption of symbolic processes. Now, the persistent question must be finally addressed: Can contemporary ideological formations and associated psychopathology be directly attributed to desymbolization (or deterritorialization) and the colonization of the lifeworld?

Important moves towards theoretical closure on this matter are provided in a thought-provoking article by Livesay (1985). Livesay argues that Habermas's attention to the abstract or formal features of intersubjective understanding and interactive competence – the thrust of most of his recent work – needs to be complemented by an analysis of psychodynamic barriers that prevent the institutionalization of capacities for communication and empathy.

> Although he rhetorically acknowledges the importance of the negative dimension of modernity, Habermas has failed to recognize the adverse impact of modern forms of differentiation and the colonization of the lifeworld on the degree of ego strength necessary to sustain a social order based upon intersubjective recognition and genuine communication.
>
> (Livesay 1985: 78)

In short, most of the subjects produced by the enculturation and socialization in advanced capitalist society are not psychologically prepared for participation in the democratization of social spheres currently dominated primarily by social steering media such as the police, the commercial news, advertising, educational and personality testing, social welfare bureaucracies, private banks, quality circles, and so forth.

Livesay asserts that the contemporary syndrome of narcissism neatly symbolizes modernity's impact since it involves numerous psychological mechanisms that interfere with capacities for more fully symbolized relatedness to others and communicative competence.

> Virtually all of the crucial features of narcissism undermine the preconditions for intersubjective recognition.... [The narcissistic] cycle of emptiness, envy, rage, devaluation and reproduced emptiness renders genuine intersubjectivity impossible and prevents the attitude of openness toward the perspective of the other.
>
> (Livesay 1985: 80)

Livesay argues further that the narcissistic style derives from a failure to de-idealize and differentiate self- and other-representations. The inability to see others realistically and to emotionally distinguish self from other 'constitutes a shaky foundation on which to build the skills of empathic role-taking, openness to the truth claims of the other, communicative competence, and intersubjective recognition' (Livesay 1985: 85). These skills are all competencies that Habermas sees as essential to decolonization and democratization. Since we are already familiar with this portrait of narcissistic traits, we need to consider the manner in which Livesay attempts to link narcissistic psychopathology to the social conditions of late capitalism. In other words, how does this particular social system manage to produce exactly the sort of personality style that supports and maintains the system rather than calling it into question and transforming it?

Following Habermas, Livesay first seeks the social origins of the narcissistic personality style in the basic contradiction between system and lifeworld in advanced capitalism. In the sphere of personality formation (socialization), the effective social contradiction is between 'popular expectations of the achievement of autonomous ego identity, on the one hand, and the systemic undermining of the ego strength necessary to sustain this developmental level of identity, on the other' (ibid.: 83).

This undermining is attributed to systemic features I have touched on several times before, including 'dependency fostered by private ownership and control of the means of production, the hierarchical division of labor, the administered policy, and the structural limits imposed on social action by the logic of the market' (ibid.). Livesay points out that these social forms are experienced contradictorily because a cultural ethic of self-determination and personal responsibility for achievement clashes with real experiences of dependency and failure that, according to the ethic, must be attributed to personal defects.

I would add that this is not merely a matter of the system promising more than it can deliver. The modern individual is hindered first of all by socialization within an impoverished lifeworld. Personality structures characterized by a lack of differentiation of images of self and other do not sustain the autonomous action and self-reflection necessary to live up to the questionable individualist ideal of the self-made man (sic). The 'self-made men' of capitalism are neither self-made nor autonomous. They are produced by the system to serve the system and generally achieve what they do through blatant exploitation of others and lack of self-understanding. The problem is not simply behavioural. Their behaviour is conditioned by an ideological process in which expectations and objective possibilities clash at the cultural level, while at the psychic level a drive for acceptance and status prevents recognition of the external contradiction.

Remembering to keep in mind the symbolic–ideological structures that mediate socialization processes, we can ask how this contradiction affects children during the process of socialization to see the genesis of the narcissistic style. Livesay is quick to point to the function of contemporary parenting styles in reinforcing the contradiction between the social ideal of permanent achievement and limited chances for success:

> Insofar as many people must cope with a disjunction between their aspirations and their achievements, vicarious participation in the successes of their children becomes one way of extending the possibilities of their own achievement. These parents both instill a sense of grandiose possibility and specialness in their children who are supposed to accomplish what their parents never could and cause their children to feel rejected since their parents' interest in them is not genuine but rather motivated by their own personal concerns.
>
> (Livesay 1985: 84)

This portrayal would not describe all families, of course, but, given a socio-economic context in which competition and status are always at issue, there is no way for a child to escape conditioning by this symbolic dimension. In families that produce narcissistic styles, the societal contradiction finds expression in contradictory parental attitudes towards their children – admiration combined with envy, false enthusiasm – setting up a scenario in which the child's narcissistic grandiosity serves as a defence against depression and a sense of meaninglessness (cf. also Sennett and Cobb 1973; Kovel 1981, 1988; Cushman 1990). An ideologically induced desymbolization ensues. The psyches of such children would be hindered both in self–other differentiation and de-idealization by the absence of non-enmeshing relations with their parents against a cultural backdrop of TV superheroes and superstars.

The narcissistic personality style is but one of many styles that can be linked to a general process of defensive desymbolization. We should thus view it as just one example of the extent to which socio-cultural contradictions mobilize psychic defences and, consequently, undermine capacities for self-understanding and mature relatedness. Having linked narcissism to both parenting styles and cultural expectations, it remains to be shown how capitalist modernization might be implicated in this scenario. In other words, would we not find similar cultural and psychological contradictions in any society characterized by class inequality?

To establish further connections between capitalist social forms and psychopathology, Livesay points to numerous links between the colonization of the lifeworld, particularly the extension of social steering media into the lifeworld, and the establishment of narcissistic defences. Recall that the uncoupling of system from lifeworld occurred in the interest of greater efficiency in production. Later, it provided new mechanisms for social control through bureaucratization of individual–state relations, policing, welfare systems and other systematic extensions of political power into the sphere of the lifeworld. The folding back of system on to lifeworld is the primary scene in which the ideological process of desymbolization can be detected. Much of this is due to the fact that social action begins to be governed by media other than symbolic communication. A certain desubjectification occurs when one becomes a human part of a mechanical process, a file in a bureaucracy, a mere provider of labour power at a certain rate per hour, a patient in a doctor's office. The co-ordination of action through such steering mechanisms tends to cut off the need for linguistic expression and intersubjective communication. This can be seen immediately in responses to protest in any of these spheres. The boss says, 'Get back to work or lose your job'. The doctor just wants straight answers to his questions about symptoms. The bureaucrat may apologize for the inconveniences of the system but nevertheless sends you on to the next office where you need to get another stamp on your papers. Thus, rather than preserving spaces in which interactions are mediated by fuller forms of communication, including protest, the colonization of the lifeworld by delinguistified steering mechanisms closes them off. The reduction of complexity is, indeed, the purpose of such steering media. Responses must be standardized to simplify the task of social control (Livesay 1985).

Life history research repeatedly shows that by the time adulthood is attained, the poverty of socially available discourses for understanding the social contradictions one has been subjected to makes it difficult for even fairly reflective individuals to piece together a coherent account of their choices and changes (Wiersma 1988). To the extent that this confusion is shared by large groups of social actors, one can assume that it serves to stabilize the existing socio-economic system. The system pays for the absence of co-ordinated protest, however, in that it must make do with an emotionally disabled citizenry.

> The strategic goals of narcissistic ego defenses produce consequences which serve to stabilize the system of advanced capitalism – in particular, by stimulating consumerist behavior designed to compensate for

the psychic experience of inner emptiness and by discouraging political activism among people more concerned about healing their doubts about themselves than about transforming social institutions.

(Livesay 1985: 87–88)

Can it be said that the creation of narcissistic structures and other neuroses is created by the socio-economic system intentionally? Definitely not. It is more accurate to say that an unintended byproduct of capitalist modernization's impact on the lifeworld is widespread neurotic functioning of various sorts, and that socially shared neuroses have tended to feed right back into system reproduction because the system itself is driven by the very motives around which the neuroses are organized: status and power (i.e. domination). Still following Livesay's argument (and many sociological studies), we may note that as modernization proceeds, status is determined less by tradition than by the logics of the market and bureaucratic power. Those who are competent in satisfying the requirements of the market and the bureaucratic structure attain status. There are many ways to accomplish this, many available roles, but competition is tough and the great majority of persons in any given generation cannot get anywhere close to expected levels of wide recognition or importance in a field of endeavour. Nevertheless, the culture industry hammers away on the self-esteem dimension by broadcasting the system of status-defining codes and signs for youth and adults to use as they organize their identities and social roles in relation to the status system.

The status system of capitalist class society is problematic for several reasons. Livesay mentions that it tends to silence those without status, rewards appearance rather than substance, reinforces narcissistic styles and encourages status competition rather than dialogue and consensus formation. Codes of status themselves become delinguistified steering media. They catch subjects from behind in early socialization, constrain communicative action and fuel compulsive system-serving cravings for money and/or power.

Examining the symbolic and ideological dimensions of socialization and enculturation in conjunction with an analysis of the contemporary situations of individuals and families appears to get us much further than unilinear and objectivistic characterizations of modernity's impact. Livesay's essay probably overemphasizes the constraining aspects of modernization, neglecting certain liberating deterritorializing processes. Furthermore, he tends to confuse the narcissistic defensive manoeuvres to which moderns resort with the more specific pathology of the narcissistic character. Yet, as he pulls together the various strands of his argument, he exemplifies the sort of analysis I have come to see as necessary:

The colonization of the lifeworld is *both* a necessary attempt to reduce the system's environmental complexity *and* a subversion of the capacities of the lifeworld to reproduce itself symbolically. Neurotic character structure represents the operation of this crisis logic at the level of personality.... Narcissistic character structures *both* reproduce the system of advanced capitalism through the depoliticization and status commodification of behavior *and* undermine the productivist mentality of capitalist culture, subvert the possibilities of achieving rational legitimating consensuses, and render people increasingly and dangerously incompetent in the face of a system which generates and is sustained by their limited competence.

(Livesay 1985: 89–90)

This perspective entails far-reaching implications for each component of the lifeworld as well as for characteristics of the system itself. The achievement of de-ideologization at the individual and collective levels will depend to a great extent on the radical modification of early socialization practices. These must be modified to encourage the development of personality structures capable of eventually transcending sadomasochistic and authoritarian impulses as well as establishing adequate self–other differentiation as the basis for genuine empathy and mutual recognition. The social institutions and practices spawned by capitalist modernization and saturated by institutionalized status competition and antidemocratic principles must be transformed. The cultural idealization of cognitive-instrumental rationality and devaluation of expressive and ethical modes of reasoning must be challenged. The paradox remains, however, that while the system must be subjected to guidance by as fully democratic processes of decision-making as practically possible, capitalist modernization has damaged psychic life to the point that the communicative capacities necessary for social transformation are in scarce supply.

Chapter 8

Decolonization

La psychologie ne détient nullement le 'secret' des faits humains, simplement parce que ce 'secret' n'est pas d'ordre psychologique.

(Psychology does not hold the 'secret' of human events, because that 'secret' is simply not of a psychological order.)

(Georges Politzer 1947: 120)

What, finally, is the problem with modernity? How can we best characterize the crisis of the modern psyche?

From the perspective of the critical psychologist, the problem could be stated as follows: The modernization of corporate capitalist societies generates a continuous ideological structuring of cultural processes, social institutions and socialization practices. This structuring, which stems from state and market operations related to social control and the maximization of profits, is accomplished through the incursion of instrumental, objectifying practices into spheres of life where other communicative processes previously prevailed. In particular, the symbolically mediated spheres of culture, society and personality are deformed by this ideological process in ways that interfere with the development and practice of individual capacities for relatedness to others, intersubjective communication and critical self-understanding. At the collective level, institutional spaces in which alternative social forms and personal identities might be envisaged and implemented are rapidly eroded and replaced by systems controlled by concentrated economic and political power.

Even if this assessment of the situation is basically correct, I suppose one must still decide if this is really a problem. In other words, might there not be more important things to worry about? One can decide if this scenario constitutes a problem only through reference to systems of values. Some values and outcomes that accompany the private and corporate accumulation of capital are not necessarily noxious: efficiency, planning, improved goods and services. The importance of these values to the smooth functioning of social and personal life is obvious to anyone who has spent much time in less 'modernized' countries, swerving to avoid long-neglected potholes, standing in long lines to accomplish the simplest of errands, accommodating to pseudo-shortages of essential goods, waiting hours for a dial-tone, and so forth.

If, however, one also values the enlightened self-determination of individuals and communities, based on respect for the basic rights of others and balanced by a well-considered awareness of personal needs, then the scenario created by capitalist forms of modernization is indeed problematic. From the perspective of a citizen of the world in the late twentieth century, that is, one who is aware of conditions in capitalist societies that include state-sponsored genocide and rampant human rights abuses, robotic consumerism and associated ecological destruction, malnourishment and starvation in the midst of plenty, and serious neglect of the educational and emotional needs of at least one billion children, the sense that modern society is in crisis cannot be written off as merely a function of arbitrary values. In fact, the values of individual and community self-determination and respect for human rights find solid grounding in humanity's historical search for a just social order. These values also inspire an emotional urgency based on compassion for the contemporary plight of fellow human beings, hopes for the happiness of future generations, and more specific concerns stemming from experiences of suffering in communities with which one feels a special connection.

What about the global trend towards capitalism? The September 1993 edition of the newsletter *Imprimis* carries the headline 'Three Cheers for Capitalism'. In the lead article, Malcolm Forbes, Jr writes, in a mode that is now all too familiar:

> Capitalism works better than any of us can conceive. It is the only truly *moral* system of exchange. It encourages individuals to freely devote their energies and impulses to peaceful pursuits, to the satisfaction of others' needs and wants, and to constructive action for the welfare of all.... Capitalism is a moral system if only because it is based on *trust*.

Assuming that most readers who have stayed with me thus far will be equally nauseated by this hypocrisy, I will not cite the article any further. It is worth noting, however, in case some of us are beginning to doubt what we plainly see, that the contemporary hype surrounding the relative success of capitalist economic practices in fostering 'growth' is already questionable on economic grounds (Fröbel *et al.* 1985; Heilbroner 1993) and in view of ecological damage related to uncontrolled development (Bahro 1986; Bookchin 1986; Gorz 1980; Ekins 1992). The celebration would instantly subside if the cheerleaders for capitalism were forced to factor into their equations the degree of human suffering attributable to capitalist development. I refer to both physical and emotional suffering at the capitalist periphery in the Third World and formerly socialist countries (Brunner 1987; Ennew and Milne 1990; Sloan 1990; Ekins 1992) as well as at the core in the cities, suburbs and rural areas of Western Europe and North America (Narr 1985; Hayes 1989; Kovel 1988; Wachtel 1989). It is hard to predict how the 'new world economic order' and 'structural adjustment' in the Third World will affect levels of suffering, but to the extent that the logic of capital accumulation prevails, further colonization of the lifeworld is to be anticipated, along with the collapse of state-sponsored safety nets for the economically disadvantaged.

Even if we stretch our minds to imagine that the basic needs of humanity might soon be met by the machinations of capitalist market forces, the systematic production of meaninglessness and psychopathology will still need to be addressed and should, in fact, become a higher priority on the socio-political agenda. I would argue, however, that we cannot wait to begin to take human needs into account in either the material or psychocultural realms. The current pessimism on the left is not justified; alternatives exist. As Trainer argues in his review of theories of economic development,

> Most development theorists, radical as well as conventional, recommend acceptance of decades of further suffering on the part of billions of people until trickle-down saves them or capitalism self-destructs, essentially because they do not understand the abundance, scope and potential of existing alternatives.
>
> (Trainer 1989: 508)

Trainer goes on to argue that the viability of post-capitalist social systems will depend less on technical and economic advances than on psychological and cultural factors such as a commitment to collective welfare, personal growth and the protection of global and local ecosystems. Lummis (1991) makes a similar point when he demonstrates that capitalist economic development is essentially an antidemocratic process.

GLOBAL AND LOCAL IMPLICATIONS

What are the alternatives to capitalist modernization? What paths come to light from the perspective of critical psychology? How might the decolonization of the lifeworld be advanced?

When the practical options available to the global citizen at this juncture are considered, the path is not as clear as one would hope. Certain possibilities for change seem promising, particularly at the individual and community levels. But just as modernity embodies numerous zones of ambiguity, so does each of the strategies that might be developed to confront capitalist modernization and foster alternative forms of social development. This fact leaves me in a delicate situation. I have often been criticized by students and colleagues for laying out depressing social scenarios and refusing to suggest remedies. At the same time, certain activist friends of mine shudder at the idea of listing concrete possibilities for action, in part because they fear that guidelines will be adopted uncritically or imposed in authoritarian moves, rather than permitting the self-organizing processes that are essential for democratic action. My decision to proceed with a consideration of various problem areas and related practical strategies should be evaluated in the context of what I have been arguing throughout the book, that is, that movements towards social transformation must strive to actualize in their own internal organization the ideals they hope to foster in the larger society.

In the following three sections I examine a variety of promising and intriguing proposals bearing on the decolonization of the lifeworld. In general, these proposals address spheres of social life that need attention if the predominance of system imperatives over the lifeworld is ever to be reversed. For purposes of clarity, I have divided these proposals according to the structural components of the lifeworld to which they are most relevant. Each proposal, however, bears at least indirectly on the other two lifeworld components and also has implications for transformation of the economy and the development of technology.

Personality and the formation of identity

In Chapter 1, I presented a vignette of an imaginary young New Yorker who exemplifies some of the identity issues associated with advanced capitalism. His difficulties with concentration, motivation and intimacy are symptoms of a life trajectory mediated by a long chain of disruptions in the social and cultural spheres. As he turns to conduct his social relationships and develop his personal projects in a manner that makes sense or feels meaningful, his already problematic expectations are met neither by the cultural nor institutional contexts that might resolve his dilemmas.

To interpret the young man's current situation, it is crucial to remember that both symbolic and practical contexts must be considered and that both have been mediating his stance towards life since birth. In other words, the actions of caretakers, teachers and friends, the content of television programmes and commercials, material studied in school, tasks required of him at work – all of these concrete aspects of life historical experience only mean what they do for him *as they are experienced symbolically* against the backdrop of the lifeworld. In his case, the relative absence of meaning and commitment might be attributed to extensive desymbolized zones of experience in connection with creative activity and intimacy. One can therefore imagine him reporting to a therapist to complain of a sense of emptiness, deadness or boredom. Having only objectivistic modes of reasoning available to him, he might request medication, hypnosis or decide he needs to change jobs.

To reiterate the problem abstractly: the colonization of the personality component of the lifeworld produces various forms of psychopathology and identity crises because it interferes with the early formation of the psyche, erodes institutional foundations for norms and values shared by the individual and replaces symbolic cultural sources of meaning with mere stimulation. Decolonization of this sphere would require that ideological desymbolization be countered by de-ideologizing resymbolization.

Several strategies suggest themselves in this connection. One could begin by fostering capacities for intersubjectivity and alternative social vision in the next generation. The decolonization of the lifeworld will depend on modifications of early socialization to promote the formation of personality structures characterized by adequate self–other differentiation and de-idealization. As Chapter 4 suggests, these structures are prerequisites to empathy, democratic attitudes and self-awareness. The more abundant these qualities in a populace, the less pleasure citizens will find in the manipulation and control of others and the more difficult it will be for states to secure power through torture, fear and propaganda. One would also expect greater sensitivity to the need to negotiate on a fairly continuous basis a balance between personal needs and collective requirements as well as a willingness to work towards a pluralistic consensus in as many spheres of life as necessary.

Addressing concerns parallel to mine, Craib examined the implications of object-relations theory for social organization and comes to similar conclusions. First, he describes the traits of a self which would be better suited to our times than the predominant forms of personality:

> Object-relations theory offers an 'ideal', a developed self, sufficiently strong to allow and tolerate strong feelings, which will often be unpleasant feelings of dependence and anger, if not hatred, without acting immediately or blindly on these feelings. The self will have a reasonably firm sense of its own boundaries, an ability to test reality and measure phantasy against reality and an ability to work creatively in an intermediate world between internal and external reality.
>
> (Craib 1990: 198–199)

Craib points out that this would not be a perfect self, but at least it would be a self less inclined to project unacceptable parts of the self on to others (as a function of stereotyped impulses). Such a self also would be less prone to get caught up in the dominance-submission axis of social relations. What forms of social organization would encourage the development of such a self? Craib answers:

> In the first case they involve arrangements which allow good-enough

mothering (and fathering) without creating disadvantages in other spheres of life for those who do become 'ordinary devoted parents'. Such arrangements clearly do not exist now. I think it also implies what we might call the continuation of parenting through school, perhaps with more real day-to-day involvement of parents with education, so that a full and complex, rather than a comparatively fragmented, external ego is there to be perceived, understood and internalised.

(Craib 1990: 199)

To bring about desired changes, adults will have to build consciously a richer repertoire of cultural images of what society might instead be like. Workable visions of non-consumerist and non-individualistic utopias are desperately needed. As Marcuse (1964) argued, the desire for social change is hindered by media announcements that Utopia has already arrived and that anyone who serves the system will reap the benefits. To break the chain of slavery, adults who are sick of the current dystopia should consider working with children to fortify alternative dreams. Since the details of such dreams need to be formulated actively in specific contexts, a promising strategy is to trust the process by which values are transmitted from one generation of progressives to the next and to ensure that children get the message that diversity is desirable and that social change is necessary. This message sets up the possibility for imagining alternative ways of doing things.

In practical terms, children need to have ongoing contact with a wide variety of caretakers, teachers, citizens and workers who take care to explain their own worlds to children through the lens of their own values. Caretakers would also emphasize learning through experience and activity, not only in day care centres and schools but also out in the city and the countryside. Such exposure to various modes of adult being as well as physical and cultural places would foster a richer sense of life options as well as the integration of lifestyle choices with better articulated values.

A tricky part of this strategy is to avoid indoctrination, which sets up empty learning and eventual rebellion or reactive conformity. It is also difficult to find an appropriate balance between individual and collective values as we shift away from the self-centred ethic. But given the distance still to be travelled – particularly in the United States – this may be a minor concern. The first task is to mobilize *social* conceptions of identity. As Poole writes,

[It] is necessary that individuals make some progress towards a social conception of their identity, if social struggle towards an alternative form of society is to be either effective or worthwhile. If it is to be effective, it will be because individuals have been willing to subordinate those goods they are able to achieve as individuals to goods which they are only able to achieve through collective action. They must find their own fulfillment in participating in that action.

(Poole 1991: 155)

The capacity to subordinate self-centred striving in this manner derives from moral development beyond that associated with narcissism and other psychopathology.

Another approach to decolonization at the personal level involves the recovery of the body. This issue is central in the work of Foucault (Rabinow 1984; Miller 1993) and French feminists such as Kristeva and Irigaray (cf. Best and Kellner 1991; Elliott, 1992). Certain forms of art and cultural practice that involve the body, such as dance and mime, have the potential to reduce alienation from the body and to bolster an awareness of unacknowledged emotional states by helping us to get 'out of our heads'. In connection with this theme, I have mixed feelings about regimented exercise, particularly when it aims primarily at developing outward attractiveness or military *esprit de corps*. Yet forms of spontaneous physical movement such as those associated with most sports may prove essential as work becomes more sedentary and urban stress more ubiquitous. As the prevalence of psychosomatic illness indicates, modern lifestyles exact a certain price at the level of the body. For example, physical anthropologists have noted that the emotional tension of urban industrial life has produced habitual malposture of the head, labelled by Hiernaux (1984) as a 'hate' posture, with the tight neck and hunched shoulders expressing insecurity or repressed aggression.

The problem in this area is to find ways of experiencing embodiment without objectifying our bodies, as in 'I'm now taking my body out for a walk' or simply buying into one of the new lifestyle products for the body's health. It cannot be denied that exercise machines increase physical health, but I wonder if they're worth the expense when the psychological consequences of the exercise scene are taken into account. Whether alone or at the health club, the exerciser's mind slips into wondering how he must look to observers. One could argue that fitness clubs are new forms of community, but I doubt that much goes on that contributes to the development of the sort of society that will foster healthier forms of relatedness. In the fitness movement I sense primarily an intensification of body-objectification, in relation to one's own body and those of others. Apart from realistic concerns about improving health and longevity, this can only be a symptom of spreading narcissism and related sexism.

Regarding the ambiguous role of psychotherapy as a mode of resymbolization in the context of capitalism, I refer readers to the excellent work by Kovel (1981, 1988), Frosh (1987) and Barratt (1988, 1993). There are clearly ways to do therapy that merely reinforce ideological desymbolization and others that encourage work on the emotional and life-historical obstacles to de-ideologization. Unfortunately, the latter sort is hard to find even among psychoanalytically oriented therapists.

Much more could be said in this section, but I prefer not to encourage excessive attention to the individual psyche and the potential for personal development apart from institutional transformation. In fact, when pushed to describe progressive activities open to psychologists, I refer not to individual or group therapy, but to community level participatory development projects of the sort carried out in Latin America (Sloan 1990).

Institutions and the sense of community

The dilemmas of the Venezuelan man I described in Chapter 1 are more typical of the vast majority of humanity than the New Yorker's. He has little time for psychological complaints. He is confronted by practical concerns that arise as he tries to survive materially in a society undergoing economic transformation. In the case of Venezuela, this process has been accelerated 'artificially' by a natural abundance of petroleum and other minerals. No longer able to survive as a subsistence farmer, as his parents did, he enters an agricultural proletariat managed poorly by administrators in the capital. As a child he was prepared culturally and psychologically for a life of hard work and responsibility as a member of the community. Now the community is fragmented by frequent labour migration. Only the elderly and the young children are regularly present. Where co-operation once characterized relations among men, competition and secrecy now prevail as individuals seek to improve their private lot and leave the rest in the dust. The pride and dignity of the elder campesinos stands in contrast to the younger ones who know the glitter of city life and look down on the simple ways of their fathers.

The state is aware of these conditions and routinely sends community workers, usually urban college students, to help organize the campesinos. Many projects have succeeded for a brief time, only to fail after the students withdrew. Politicians also arrive regularly at election time and promise improvements: better homes, sewers, roads, clinics. Expecting at least something to get better, the people vote and wait. If they leave, they join the ranks of the urban poor in objectively worse conditions. If they stay, they risk falling further behind as their way of life and the culture that integrated home life and production become increasingly obsolete. Given their socialization in the Christian value of charity, the young men and women who recognize the rural stalemate are quick to understand the guerrilla's calls for land reform, collective ownership of the means of production, redistribution of wealth and real educational opportunities for all. They also cannot mistake the élite's alliance with the military and the police. Caught between the collapse of traditional institutions on the one hand and the faltering development of modern ones on the other, the Venezuelan man in question has nowhere to go.

The uncoupling of system from lifeworld and subsequent capitalist modernization take a heavy toll on the quality of formal and informal institutional life. Flows of capital, supplanting individual and collective aspirations, tear up the social landscape. Feelings of neighbourhood and sense of place fade as bureaucratic rationalization and market forces inspire the anonymity of federal buildings, residential subdivisions, shopping malls and freeways. Workshops, classrooms and offices increasingly screen out activities not directly relevant to productivity. Homes are parcelled up into private compartments for passive reception of entertainment. These 'external' changes have psychological repercussions. A sense of place is not only about being in a familiar place. It is about understanding those around one and being aware of previous generations who settled the place. Although modern nomadic life teaches us that identities can be formed that have little relation to place, I know few nomads who will not admit that they are in fact looking for 'home' or that they wish they had roots. To substitute for homes and roots, work or leisure identities provided by the system are tried out. These are not especially satisfying for people whose identities are not predominantly organized to serve the system's needs for production, consumption and status games. Anomie and political apathy flourish.

De-ideologization at the level of social institutions will require multiple strategies, each of which risks co-optation. A fairly obvious strategy is to develop institutions and practices that counter the tendency towards isolation and restore a sense of place. This proposal encourages maximal interaction, involvement and understanding across age, gender and ethnic divides. Such interaction can be stimulated by practical measures such as housing, schooling and employment arrangements that simultaneously reduce community-disrupting geographic mobility and affirm both diversity and participation.

A prime concern here is the geographic mobility of parents that, especially in the United States, leaves suburban youth without a sense of place or community. This trend will be difficult to reverse until there are reasons to attach to one's neighbourhood in the first place. Planners have recently realized that the anonymity and sterility of suburban communities can be counteracted somewhat by planning zones of concentration – other than the shopping malls – where people rediscover small town feeling in the place where the post office, town hall, cultural centre and other buildings can be reached on foot. The success of such plans will depend on there being something other than shopping to do in these new centres.

In this regard, a study by Fernandez-Christlieb (1991) is noteworthy. He notes that modernization gradually eliminates public spaces for conversation and debate (the plaza, the pub, the dining room) leaving open primarily those channels of communication that foster ideological programming (television, public administration) and repetitious inward conversation or self-talk (the bathroom, the single-occupant apartment).

At the international level, repatriation of exiles and refugees should be supported where it is desired and conditions that stimulate economic migration need to be confronted aggressively to reduce psychocultural dislocation (Carstairs 1984; Yeh 1985). Human beings are incredibly adaptive, but when possibilities for reconnection with original lifeways and renewal of familiar lifeworld processes exist, they should be supported financially by governments and international organizations.

The key dimension of strategies designed to decolonize this component of the lifeworld is the restoration of communication. In advanced capitalism there is plenty of communication, but it flows in one direction. As Narr puts it:

> [It] is clear that the direction and driving force determining the development of information, of the media, and of the various forms of communication – from the telephone to wideband communication to automated subways – are based not on the individual's needs, potentials, or social organization but on the imperatives of a logic of capital realization. . . . Individuals possess no controlling criteria, no controlling information, no controlling communication.
>
> (Narr 1985: 43)

The problem is not only that moderns (or postmoderns actually) are overwhelmed with information and a multitude of relationships, as Gergen (1991) has demonstrated. The problem is that so little can be done with the types of information and modes of communication to which we have access. This is basically a failure to actualize the ideal of democracy. The strategic intention must therefore be to extend participation and democratic process to all spheres of life. If modernization is in part a process that increasingly excludes people from participation in the decisions that determine the form of their social order, it is imperative to reverse the trend of 'departicipation' (Gran 1983). Power and wealth can only be decentralized by insisting on organizational procedures that favour decision-making based on participatory consensus formation rather than hierarchically exercised authority. To offset political colonialism and postcolonialism associated with economic dependency, participatory democratic and grassroots organizations of communities should determine local and regional economic policy and work to facilitate the acquisition of benefits of modernity that facilitate further participation: better mass transit, telephones, primary health care, and education (Ekins 1992).

The drive for democratization relies not only on institutional procedures and norms that require input from all concerned, but also on

individual capacities for participation and the intergenerational transmission of cultural understandings that hold democracy as an ideal. If the
theme of democracy sounds clichéd, it is only because in the context of
capitalist societies, democratic elections have been reduced to a competition between relatively similar positions. Perhaps a new word should be
devised to refer to the process of reaching a consensus through equal
participation in dialogue between all parties involved. In the context of
this book, the term de-ideologization comes close, but it is obviously too
awkward, just as these processes will be in any sphere where they are
newly initiated.

Culture and the restoration of meaning

The situation of the young Egyptian woman described in Chapter 1
reveals certain dimensions of the colonization of the lifeworld in the
sphere of culture. The rift she experiences between her parents' expectations and her own lifestyle preferences is a direct product of the penetration of foreign capital into her country. The state facilitates the process
by instituting mass secular education and exchange programmes with
European capitals. Soon the market is flooded not only with essential
commodities but also with European and North American cultural products backed by powerful advertising (films, dance music, bestselling
books). As she looks for images around which to consolidate an identity
that expresses her differences with her parents' restricting views of
womanhood, Madonna's feisty style fits the bill. For some of her friends
in engineering school, simply wearing Western dress and pursuing a tra-
ditionally male career is challenge enough to the old order. But this
woman's experience includes witnessing her father verbally abusing her
mother through the years and her own contrasting summer vacation
romance with a gentle punk rocker in Paris. She thus feels most at home
in the discothèques and record stores of Cairo, sites that have little to do
with Egypt. Perhaps the gap between her reception of the international
pop music culture and the local practices she finds herself defending when
abroad is indicated by her daydreams. She imagines putting classical
Arabic love poetry to Madonna-style music and making music videos for
local consumption.

The colonization of the culture component of the lifeworld undermines
traditional sources of meaning and the transmission of cultural knowledge
relevant to individual and collective well-being. The resulting deficit is not
met adequately by the deluge of information technologies, bureaucratic
structures and educational institutions.

As Poster (1990) suggests, however, post-industrial communications
technologies and the modernizing messages they carry have the potential
to play at least a facilitating role in extending the beneficial aspects of

modernity to larger sectors. The young Egyptian's situation reminds one that the contents and effects of lifeworld processes, in her case, the social legitimation of patriarchal authority, are not always such that one would choose to defend them from systemic rationalization through, for example, equal rights legislation. This point is developed by Fraser (1989) in a feminist critique of Habermas's hopes for restored communicative action grounded in vibrant lifeworld contexts. If the symbolic processes of the lifeworld are organized phallocentrically, should women attempt to reverse or hinder their disruption by the system? I would argue that the point of decolonizing the lifeworld is not to preserve specific cultural contents such as role expectations and gender norms, but to create spaces in which identities and institutions can be transformed through self-reflection, intersubjective communication and social action. Whether such transformation actually occurs will depend simultaneously on participants' preparedness for the challenges of egalitarian relations and on development of institutional structures that support democratic consensus formation rather than autocratic decision-making.

In the final analysis, decolonization of the cultural sphere will depend in large part on delinking cultural activity from the marketing of commodities. Forms of cultural resistance adequate to new communications media and the internationalization of capital will need to be invented. Cultural meanings will begin to flourish anew in conjunction with this resistance and related institutional transformation, just as the struggles of previous generations of activists and dissidents motivate contemporary efforts.

In conjunction with the foregoing, artistic expression itself needs to be affirmed more as a source of insight and critique for all citizens. The proposal here is not for more art history courses or more finger painting and clay play, but rather to encourage and develop artistic sensibilities and skills in every individual. If some degree of artistic expression were a possibility for everyone, the tendency to mystify and commodify art would decline. The inclination to stand back and admire art or music, rather than participate in its creation, would also be weakened. It is difficult to see why art deserves attention when so many apparently more pressing problems are at hand. The answer is related to psychological factors, not the least of which is the need to keep hope and critical understanding alive. Stephen White explains this well:

> [W]hat exactly is there in the modern aesthetic experience which allows the accumulation of some sort of insight? Apparently, the key is greater fluidity and flexibility in modes of access to our desires and feelings. The radical decoupling of the aesthetic sense from the imperatives of society and tradition has the potential for informing consciousness about how we normally interpret our desires and feelings in ways

which unreflectively mirror the prevailing value standards of the culture around us.

(White 1988: 149)

Debates will always rage about what sorts of art, and what kinds of relations we develop to it, might best achieve such effects as well as about whether artists should intentionally strive to play an emancipatory role, but I think the basic argument here is sound: artistic processes, apart from being inherently enjoyable, are linked to processes of self-knowledge and communication that are essential to personal and social transformation.

I hesitate to comment on the issue of television, but I will suggest that it may be time to start a social experiment to unplug the child and the adult from media-provided pseudo-information, packaged images of selfhood, vacuous entertainment, etc. This would involve turning off the television as much as possible and allowing ourselves to see what we do instead. Quite a lot of people already do this. Many of these are readers who never wanted a television or who realized that television watching in general was not improving the quality of their lives. This is not to say that television must go entirely. It should be possible to control time spent with the television, emphasizing the selection of programmes that are worth watching and perhaps limiting it to a certain number of hours per week, as many families have had to do with their children. Of course, no one could dictate a priori what is worth watching. Communication among family members about ridiculous television content may make the watching of even the worst shows productive.

In terms of community strategy, it is important to support democratic-ally-controlled local television and radio programming to dilute cultural imperialism of the transnational media conglomerates (see Mattelart 1983). The new technologies can be put to work to decrease the distance between expert knowledge and citizen understanding. The more such technologies are in the hands of local communities, the more political space will exist for the creative preservation and development of cultural identities challenged by globalization and commodification (van Nieuwen-huijze 1984; Gibbons 1985). This point is particularly relevant to indus-trializing societies:

> The best way to protect cultural identity which is the most vulner-able part of the edifice of most Third World countries is by making culture one of the key motors of the development process and by encouraging an endogenous and creative use of the new information technologies.

(Elmandjra 1985: 3)

Such efforts are crucial not only for the *preservation* of local culture and language, but to stimulate local participation in the primary medium that *creates* new cultural forms in the modern world. The contradiction remains, however, that while the idea here is to decrease media-packaged knowledge of the world, to know the world more directly through local and global travel, reading, and conversation with friends and strangers, certain forms of critical participation in the television medium will be necessary in order not to surrender that terrain to ideological forces.

Another principle that suggests itself here is to shift from passive spectator–consumer roles to active modes of participation. This applies to multiple spheres of cultural life: food preparation, music, sports, education, art, crafts.

Finally, the framework presented in this book would suggest the promotion of literacy in conjunction with local writing, publishing and reading. The literacy work of Paolo Freire (1981) is exemplary here. In Freire's work with campesinos, critical thinking is taught with minimal imposition of outside codes. As O'Neill describes the point of Freire's work, the process enables them to

> test the objectification of their social world against their existential experience and to reevaluate the objective institutional order in terms of subjective relevances. However, rather than devalue their own experiences in favor of the ruling codification, they judge the latter in light of the alternative community generated by critical understanding.
>
> (O'Neill 1985: 68)

LIFEWORLD OVER SYSTEM

My entire argument has been framed within a discourse of emancipation or liberation that privileges speech, dialogue and other symbolic communication as means to social transformation. Much of what I have written is addressed to people who have fairly comfortable positions, as I do, within the system that needs to be transformed. I have tried to show that being comfortable can usually be equated with being part of the problem. Since the urgency of the project of emancipation is already much clearer to those who cannot speak out or who are tortured for speaking out, I have highlighted the psychological consequences of capitalist modernization in the middle classes of the industrialized sectors. These classes do not direct the system, but they manage it and could make a big difference if they were to align with the working and marginalized classes rather than with the capitalist élite.

> Before the language of liberation can sound convincing [to those who benefit from the oppressive systems], it must be shown that 'development', as normally understood, alienates even its beneficiaries in com-

pulsive consumption, technological determinisms of various sorts, ecological pathology, and warlike policies.

(Goulet 1983: 466)

Linked to this agenda is the importance of establishing the legitimacy in academic work of what Habermas (1971) calls the emancipatory interest in knowledge-seeking. Contrasting this to the interests in technical control and historical-interpretive work, Habermas describes the emancipatory interest as

an attitude which is formed in the experience of suffering from something man-made, which can be abolished and should be abolished. This is not just a contingent value-postulate: that people want to get rid of certain sufferings. No, it is something so profoundly ingrained in the structure of human societies – the calling into question, and the deep-seated wish to throw off, relations which oppress you without necessity – so intimately built into the reproduction of human life that I don't think it can be regarded as just a subjective attitude which may or may not guide this or that piece of scientific research.

(Habermas 1986: 198)

In short, the silence surrounding the linkage between capitalist economic development and various forms of unnecessary suffering must be broken.

Essential transformation at the level of lifeworld processes will only be possible if simultaneous work is done in the political-economic sphere. In this context I can only point to some of the more obvious avenues. Consumerist investment decisions need to be criticized effectively through protest in planning stages and later through boycotts. Citizens must object to the planning of shopping malls in already over-serviced areas and the creation of 'false needs' for new products through advertising. Energy expended on producing and attracting new consumers is wasted energy. People 'have the right and the opportunity to become something else' (Dagnino 1980: 201).

Lifestyle choices are not the main issues for most of the world's population. The majority of material production of the next few decades should be shifted towards meeting the basic needs of the world's poor to reduce the gap in material standards of living and effect a redistribution of the world's wealth. Decisions to do this will not come easily: 'In a finite world there has to be global redistribution or a kind of global apartheid. In either case the result will almost certainly involve violent revolution' (Brugger 1983: 57). I am not sure about Brugger's conclusion, but the violence related to the unequal distribution of wealth has already been massive since the Second World War, in the so-called Third World wars, the crushing of labour movements, and the torture and disappearances of activists, teachers, union leaders, artists, etc. (Chailand 1978; Clark

1986; Martín-Baró 1994), not to mention the violence of everyday drudgery and poverty. The sooner the men who control the international economic order perceive this and act on their new awareness, the less violent the process of redistribution will be. As their sense of control globalizes further, however, they seem less inclined to change direction. As Guattari sees it, the 'present world crisis is directed, in the last analysis, to establishing a new method for the general economic and political subjugation of the collective labour-force all over the world' (1984: 265). DuBois (1991) establishes the same point. Put simply, the globalization of capital is harnessing and co-ordinating human energies in a totalitarian mode, all in the name of 'democracy' and 'freedom'.

Decentralization is frequently suggested these days as a way of breaking down the concentration of power in the hands of so few. This would involve the construction of 'more complex, diverse, and skilled societies of small producers, owning real property and controlling a significant body of skills' in order to 'reunify production and consumption in the same population centers' (Luke 1991: 78). To avoid manipulation of such relatively self-sufficient communities by the transnational New Class, alternative networks of communities and co-operatives will be necessary. This could be modelled on the developing communications and appropriate technology linkages within the non-profit sector in the United States or among non-governmental organizations in the Third World (Ekins 1992).

WRAP UP

As I mentioned above, I delved into these strategic issues with some trepidation. Each suggestion or proposal entails numerous side issues that need to be thought through much further in relation to specific contexts. Rather than explore nuances or discuss situational variations relevant to change strategies or tactics, I will conclude by clarifying my stance on a few points.

As we try to understand social problems that might be associated with modernization, it is essential to look at the other side of the coin, to ask ourselves whether what we perceive as a problem is really a problem or just seems to be a problem because we do not understand it. We tend to assume, on the basis of what we have associated culturally and ideologically with the Good in the Past, that changes and differences from the Good Past are Bad Futures. Contemporary examples: lesbian parents, indigenous peoples watching television, the breakdown of the extended family, voter apathy, test-tube babies, etc. This is not to deny that certain changes and differences in social behaviour may actually entail increased suffering and social conflict, but it implies that we cannot make up our minds at once about what it is that constitutes a problem. In many cases the 'problem' may be set up more by resistance from narrow-minded sectors of society than by anything inherent to the new social form.

We must therefore distinguish between countermodernization and the 'new social movements' inspired by the ideals of modernity, such as democracy and equality (White 1988), or postmodernity (multi-culturalism). Countermodernization efforts (religious fundamentalism, racist hate groups) are reactions to the passing of traditional forms due to rationalization in accordance with progressive values. They struggle to preserve previous forms of domination (for example, patriarchy or slavery). The new social movements, which include the ecology, peace, women's and human rights movements, work to protect and extend institutional spaces for expression, understanding and interaction introduced by modernization. For example, the new social movements 'protest the dependence of buyer–seller, employee–employer relationships, as well as the political dependence, passivity, and privatism fostered by client–civil servant and elector–office-holder relationships' (Ingram 1987: 165).

Modernization is not, as some would have it, merely a benign matter of cross-cultural communication or acculturation. Its impact on non-Western cultures can be devastating:

> On contact with the West, tradition changes into folklore commercialized for tourist consumption, or an ideological instrument in the service of a nationalism, or it gets lost in other syncretic forms. The West swallows up everything and leaves the other players no chance to develop an autonomous will.
>
> (Karnoouh 1984: 80; see also Alvares 1992)

Resistance to modernization is likely to be a cultural defence mechanism (Bastide 1971; Routledge 1987) or an attempt to reclaim and aggressively resymbolize a zone of the lifeworld that is being occupied. Nativism, Messianism, retribalization, millenarianism, cargo cults, etc., can thus be understood as counter-modernization measures. And as Lindstrom (1993) points out, not only non-Western societies are replete with such manifestations. Similarly, rather than blaming the victim, the epidemics of alcoholism, spouse abuse and homicide among rapidly modernizing cultural groups can be seen as consequences of social disintegration, colonization and the destruction of cultural lifeworlds (Watson 1970; Bulhan 1985).

Almost all of the proposals I mention above are designed to augment capacities and/or opportunities for the intersubjective expression and communication of needs, sufferings and visions of alternative modes of life. To some extent these opportunities can be expanded through the creation of diverse new 'political spaces' (Laclau and Mouffe 1985) in which excommunicated desires and felt needs can be articulated in speech and action. This implies work at the institutional level to allow subjects who already sense their oppression to express their demands and work to build alternative institutional forms. This is a complex matter for it has become all too clear in the twentieth century that there can be no 'master plan'. The play of power is such that there is a 'constant displacement of the nodal points structuring a social formation' (ibid.: 177). One cannot determine a priori exactly the points at which space must be opened up. But psychic suffering itself indicates points at which the communication of needs and interests must occur in order to transform relations of domination. It can be, and perhaps always has been, one of the main wellsprings of democratic principles.

In chaotic times, when power is exercised behind the scenes and there appears to be no central organizing discourse, subjects are susceptible to totalitarian movements that promise new unity, stability and meaning. As recent history amply demonstrates, such movements have only silenced individuals further and reduced collective sensitivity to the diversity of needs and aspirations among social groups. Radical democracy is thus the primary political ideal that follows from a consideration of psychological as well as material needs in the context of capitalist modernity. 'The multiplication of political spaces and the preventing of the concentration of power in one point are... preconditions of every truly democratic transformation of society' (Laclau and Mouffe 1985: 178). Many of the practical mechanisms for opening up such spaces can be linked to what Bouchier (1987) terms 'radical citizenship', a constellation of attitudes and activities that includes the themes of radical decentralism, participatory democracy, community development, pragmatic gradualism and the critique of everyday life.

Many of the strategies or proposals touched on here bear on the situation of societies that are moving into that still mysterious terrain of postmodernity or 'informational capitalism' (Luke and White 1985), while others are more relevant to industrializing societies. This dichotomy is somewhat arbitrary, of course, since some sectors of Third World societies have 'jumped' directly to social forms associated with postmodernity and large sectors of supposedly industrialized societies are still 'underdeveloped'. The diversity of my conclusions is thus intentional, for although no individual or movement could possibly be involved in actualizing them all, it is important to note how the links between apparently disparate struggles come into view when our criterion shifts towards psychological development and social justice and moves away from the imperative for capitalist economic growth. We must recognize our allies globally and locally, then co-operate energetically with them. Furthermore, although I have emphasized changes or strategies that challenge the domination of our 'inner nature', many of these go hand in hand with contemporary movements designed to protect outer nature, the environment, from industrial civilization. Personally, I would give priority to changes that directly bear on the present situation of children. As Ashis Nandy (1987) suggests, children have for far too long been the victims of adults' inability to work things out in the 'adult world' – ironically, greater mutuality with children could socialize and re-humanize adults.

Is there basis for hope? Many authors suggest that proactive movements for change tend to occur only in times of crisis. Bruce Brown explains how ideological reification, that is, the naturalization of the social order, sets up a psychological blindness to the need for change:

> People who perceive the world through the mask of reification never question the exploitative and oppressive relationships which determine their lives, for they are unable to imagine that any alternative to this situation is possible. Only during periods in which the reifying structures of institutions are disrupted – during periods of profound social crisis and disintegration – does a clear perception of the true nature of a society and the structural relationships which characterize it become fully possible.
>
> (B. Brown 1973: 12–13)

Whether or not we are now experiencing the cultural and material crisis of modernity painfully enough to get out of our chairs will depend on the particular situations in which we find ourselves.

Unfortunately, modern media have accustomed us to the sense of being constantly in crisis. We have a new media-fabricated crisis every few months. But each of us experiences contemporary crises in one realm of life or another in a privatized manner and we tend to respond to these crises as though they were personal decisions (Sloan 1987). Attention to the linkages between our personal plights and macrosocial change can be the first step towards the de-privatization needed to generate forms of solidarity with others that will make change possible. Private self-transformation is illusory. As Broughton (1986: 159) argues, 'It will take collective will, the consensual reinterpretation of our own suppressed needs, and the cautious, self-conscious reconstruction of science and society before the self can emerge in a more emancipated form in a more liberated world'.

In deciding *what* to do, it is essential to remember that the problems to be addressed flow from a failure to actualize the ethical ideal of modernity. This ideal entails an image of the value, dignity, equality and freedom of the human individual (Naumann and Hufner 1985). Capitalist forms of modernization have managed to amass the material prerequisites for the realization of the ideal of modernity, but have failed to capitalize on this possibility. Ideological lip service to the ideal has blinded many to domination and destruction of outer nature and the deformation of inner nature that results from lop-sided emphasis on instrumental rationality.

It is strange that the experience of social injustice has not been enough to mobilize the mainstream citizens of modernized societies, but now that they see their own plight reflected symbolically in the destruction of the natural environment, they may begin to question the system that threatens the sheer existence of all. Rather than despair over human shortsightedness, however, we must gather our anger and focus our individual capacities and collective energies on the decolonization of the lifeworld and the construction of a humane social order. The horrifying alternative is the spread of a social order that already mimics the gruesome techno-barbarism portrayed in all-too prophetic science fiction films.

References

Adorno, T. (1973) *Negative Dialectics*, New York: Seabury.
—— (1974) [1951] *Minima Moralia: Reflections from Damaged Life*, London: New Left Books.
—— (1982) [1951] 'Freudian theory and the pattern of Fascist propaganda', in A. Arato and E. Gebhardt (eds) *The Essential Frankfurt School Reader*, New York: Continuum, pp. 118–137.
Adorno, T., Frenkel-Brunswik, E., Levinson, D., and Sanford, R. N. (1950) *The Authoritarian Personality*, New York: Harper.
Alavi, H. and Shanin, T. (eds) (1982) *Introduction to the Sociology of 'Developing' Societies*, New York: Monthly Review Press.
Alford, C. F. (1989) *Melanie Klein and Critical Social Theory*, New Haven: Yale University Press.
—— (1991) *The Self in Social Theory*, New Haven: Yale University Press.
Al-Haj, M. (1988) 'The changing Arab kinship structure: the effect of modernization in an urban community', *Economic Development and Cultural Change* 36: 237–258.
Allingham, M. (1987) *Unconscious Contracts: A Psychoanalytical Theory of Society*, London: Routledge and Kegan Paul.
Alvares, C. (1992) *Science, Development, and Violence*, London: Oxford University Press.
Arnason, J. (1991) 'Modernity as project and field of tensions', in A. Honneth and H. Joas (eds) *Communicative Action*, Cambridge, UK: Polity Press, pp. 181–213.
Bacal, H. and Newman, K. (1990) *Theories of Object Relations: Bridges to Self Psychology*, New York: Columbia University Press.
Bahro, R. (1986) *Building the Green Movement*, Philadelphia: New Society.
Baran, P. and Sweezy, P. (1966) *Monopoly Capital*, New York: Monthly Review Press.
Barglow, R. (1994) *The Crisis of the Self in the Age of Information*, London: Routledge.
Barratt, B. (1984) *Psychic Reality and Psychoanalytic Knowing*, Hillsdale, NJ: Analytic Press.
—— (1988) 'Why is psychoanalysis so controversial? Notes from left field!', *Psychoanalytic Psychology* 5(3): 223–239.
—— (1993) *Psychoanalysis and the Postmodern Impulse: Knowing and Being Since Freud's Psychology*, Baltimore: The Johns Hopkins University Press.
Bastide, R. (1971) *Anthropologie Appliquée*, Paris: Payot.
Baudrillard, J. (1981) *For a Critique of the Political Economy of the Sign*, St Louis, MO: Telos.

Baumeister, R. (1987) 'How the self became a problem: a psychological review of historical research', *Journal of Personality and Social Psychology* 52: 163–176.

Bell, D. (1965) 'The disjunction of culture and social structure: some notes on the meaning of social reality', in G. Holton (ed.) *Science and Culture*, Boston: Houghton Mifflin, pp. 236–250.

Benhabib, S. (1986) *Critique, Norm, and Utopia*, New York: Columbia University Press.

Benjamin, J. (1977) 'The end of internalization: Adorno's social psychology', *Telos* 32: 42–64.

—— (1988) *The Bonds of Love*, New York: Basic Books.

Berger, B. (1971) *Societies in Change: An Introduction to Comparative Sociology*, New York: Basic Books.

Berger, P. (1977) *Facing Up to Modernity*, London: Penguin.

Berger, P. and Luckmann, T. (1966) *The Social Construction of Reality*, New York: Anchor.

Berger, P., Berger, B., and Kellner, H. (1974) *The Homeless Mind: Modernization and Consciousness*, New York: Vintage.

Berman, M. (1982) *All That is Solid Melts Into Air: The Experience of Modernity*, New York: Simon and Schuster.

Bernstein, R. (ed.) (1985) *Habermas and Modernity*, Cambridge: MIT Press.

Best, S. and Kellner, D. (1991) *Postmodern Theory: Critical Interrogations*, New York: Guilford.

Black, C. (1984) 'An introduction to modernization studies', in M. Nagai (ed.) *Development in the Non-Western World*, Tokyo: University of Tokyo Press, pp. 124–129.

Bleicher, J. (1980) *Contemporary Hermeneutics*, London: Routledge.

Blumer, H. (1990) *Industrialization as an Agent of Social Change: A Critical Analysis*, New York: A. de Gruyter.

Bogue, R. (1989) *Deleuze and Guattari*, London: Routledge.

Bollas, C. (1989) *Forces of Destiny*, London: Free Association.

Bookchin, M. (1986) *The Modern Crisis*, Philadelphia: New Society.

Boothby, R. (1991) *Death and Desire*, New York: Routledge.

Bottomore, T. (1983) *A Dictionary of Marxist Thought*, Cambridge, MA: Harvard University Press.

Bouchier, D. (1987) *Radical Citizenship*, New York: Schocken.

Boudon, R. (1986) *Theories of Social Change: A Critical Appraisal*, Berkeley: University of California Press.

Broughton, J. (1986) 'The psychology, history, and ideology of the self', in K. Larsen (ed.) *Dialectics and Ideology in Psychology*, Norwood, NJ: Ablex, pp. 128–164.

Broughton, J. (ed.) (1987) *Critical Theories of Psychological Development*, New York: Plenum.

Brown, B. (1973) *Marx, Freud, and the Critique of Everyday Life*, New York: Monthly Review Press.

Brown, N. O. (1959) *Life Against Death: The Psychoanalytical Meaning of History*, Middletown, CT: Wesleyan University Press.

Brown, R. (1976) *Modernization: The Transformation of American Life, 1600–1865*, New York: Hill and Wang.

Brugger, B. (1983) *Modernisation and Revolution*, Beckenham, Kent: Croom Helm.

Brunner, J. (1987) 'Los debates sobre la modernidad y el futuro de América

Latina', in G. Martner (ed.) *Diseños Para el Cambio*, Caracas: Nueva Sociedad, pp. 73–115.

Bulhan, H. (1985) *Frantz Fanon and the Psychology of Oppression*, New York: Plenum.

Cahoone, L. (1988) *The Dilemma of Modernity*, Albany: SUNY Press.

Carstairs, G. (1984) 'Mental health and the environment in developing countries', in H. Freeman (ed.) *Mental Health and the Environment*, New York: Churchill Livingstone, pp. 425–452.

Castilla del Pino, C. (1969) *Psicoanálisis y Marxismo*, Madrid: Alianza.

Chailand, G. (1978) *Revolution in the Third World*, New York: Penguin.

Chasseguet-Smirgel, J. and Grunberger, B. (1986) *Freud or Reich?: Psychoanalysis and Illusion*, London: Free Association.

Clark, R. (1986) *Power and Policy in the Third World*, New York: Macmillan.

Craib, I. (1990) *Psychoanalysis and Social theory*, Amherst: University of Massachusetts.

Cushman, P. (1990) 'Why the self is empty: toward a historically situated psychology', *American Psychologist* 45: 599–611.

Dagnino, E. (1980) 'Cultural and ideological dependence: building a theoretical framework', in K. Kumar (ed.) *Transnational Enterprises*, Boulder: Westview, pp. 297–321.

D'Amico, R. (1978) 'Desire and the commodity form', *Telos* 35: 88–122.

Deleuze, G. and Guattari, F. (1983) *Anti-Oedipus*, Minnesota: University of Minnesota Press.

Desai, A. (1976) 'Need for revaluation of the concept', in C. Black (ed.) *Comparative Modernization*, New York: Free Press, pp. 89–103.

Dilthey, W. (1961) *Pattern and Meaning in History*, New York: Harper and Row.

DuBois, M. (1991) 'The governance of the Third World: a Foucauldian perspective on power relations in development', *Alternatives* 16: 1–30.

Eagleton, T. (1991) *Ideology: An Introduction*, London: Verso.

Earnest, W. R. (1992) 'Ideology criticism and interview research', in G. Rosenwald and R. Ochberg (eds) *Storied Lives*, New Haven: Yale University Press, pp. 250–264.

Eisenstadt, S. (1973) *Tradition, Change, and Modernity*, New York: John Wiley.

Ekins, P. (1992) *A New World Order: Grassroots Movements for Global Change*, New York: Routledge.

Elias, N. (1978) *The Civilizing Process*, Vol. 1, New York: Urizen Books.

Elliott, A. (1992) *Social Theory and Psychoanalysis in Transition*, Oxford: Blackwell.

—— (1993) 'The self-destructive subject: critical theory and the analysis of the unconscious and society', *Free Associations* 3(4): 503–544.

Elmandjra, M. (1985) 'Communication, informatics and development', *Development* No. 1: 3–5.

Ennew, J. and Milne, B. (1990) *The Next Generation: Lives of Third World Children*, Philadelphia: New Society.

Erikson, E. (1950) *Childhood and Society*, New York: Norton.

Etzioni-Halevy, E. (1981) *Social Change*, London: Routledge and Kegan Paul.

Fernandez-Christlieb, P. (1991) *El Espíritu de la Calle: Psicología Política de la Cultura Cotidiana*, Guadalajara: Universidad de Guadalajara.

Fiske, D. and Shweder, R. (eds) (1986) *Metatheory in Social Science*, Chicago: University of Chicago Press.

Foucault, M. (1977) *Discipline and Punish: The Birth of the Prison*, New York: Pantheon.

Fraser, N. (1989) *Unruly Practices*, Minneapolis: University of Minnesota Press.

Freire, P. (1981) *Education for Critical Consciousness*, New York: Continuum.

Freud, S. (1958) [1911] 'Formulations on the two principles of mental functioning', in J. Strachey (ed. and trans.) *The Standard Edition of the Complete Psychological Works of Sigmund Freud* 3: 187–222, London: Hogarth Press.

—— (1958) [1930] 'Civilization and its discontents', *Standard Edition* 21 57–146.

Fröbel, F., Heinrichs, J., and Kreye, O. (1985) 'The global crisis and developing countries', in H. Addo (ed.) *Development as Social Transformation*, Boulder: Westview, pp. 111–124.

Fromm, E. (1947) *Man for Himself: An Inquiry into the Psychology of Ethics*, New York: Rinehart.

—— (1955) *The Sane Society*, New York: Rinehart.

Frosh, S. (1987) *The Politics of Psychoanalysis*, London: Methuen.

—— (1989) 'Melting into air: psychoanalysis and social experience', *Free Associations* 16: 7–30.

Garnier, J.-P. and Lew, R. (1984) 'From the wretched of the earth to the defence of the West: an essay on left disenchantment in France', in *Socialist Register 1984*, London: Merlin, pp. 299–323.

Gear, M., Hill, M., and Liendo, E. (1981) *Working Through Narcissism: Treating its Sadomasochistic Structure*, New York: Aronson.

Gergen, K. (1991) *The Saturated Self: Dilemmas of Identity in Contemporary Life*, New York: Basic Books.

Gibbons, A. (1985) *Information, Ideology and Communication: The New Nations' Perspectives on an Intellectual Revolution*, New York: University Press of America.

Gorz, A. (1980) *Ecology as Politics*, Boston: South End Press.

Goulet, D. (1983) "Development" . . . or "liberation?", in C. K. Wilbur (ed.) *Political Economy of Development and Underdevelopment*, 3rd edition, New York: Random House.

Gran, G. (1983) *Development by People: Citizen Control of a Just World*, New York: Praeger.

Greenspan, S. (1989) *The Development of the Ego*, Madison, CT: International Universities Press.

Gregg, G. (1991) *Self-Representation: Life Narrative Studies in Identity and Ideology*, New York: Greenwood.

Grotstein, J. (1991) 'Nothingness, meaninglessness, chaos, the "black hole" III', *Contemporary Psychoanalysis* 27(1): 1–33.

Guattari, F. (1984) *Molecular Revolution: Psychiatry and Politics*, Tr. R. Sheed. London: Penguin.

Habermas, J. (1970) *Toward a Rational Society*, Boston: Beacon.

—— (1971) *Knowledge and Human Interests*, Boston: Beacon.

—— (1984) *The Theory of Communicative Action*, Vol. 1, *Reason and the Rationalization of Society*, Boston: Beacon.

—— (1986) *Autonomy and Solidarity: Interviews*, London: Verso.

—— (1987) *The Theory of Communicative Action*, Vol. 2, *Life World and System*, Boston: Beacon.

—— (1990) *Moral Consciousness and Communicative Action*, Cambridge, MA: MIT Press.

Haferkamp, H. and Smelser, N. (eds) (1992) *Social Change and Modernity*, Berkeley: University of California Press.

Hannay, N. and McGuinn, R. (1980) 'The anatomy of modern technology: prolegomenon to an improved public policy for the social management of technology', *Daedalus* 109: 25–53.

Harvey, D. (1985) *Consciousness and the Urban Experience*, Baltimore: The Johns Hopkins University Press.

Hayes, D. (1989) *Behind the Silicon Curtain*, Boston: South End Press.

Heilbroner, R. (1993) *21st Century Capitalism*, New York: Norton.

Held, D. (1980) *Introduction to Critical Theory*, Berkeley: University of California Press.

Henriques, J., Hollway, W., Urwin, C., Venn, C., and Walkerdine, V. (1984) *Changing the Subject*, London: Methuen.

Hewitt, J. (1989) *Dilemmas of the American Self*, Philadelphia: Temple University Press.

Hiernaux, J. (1984) 'Natural head poise and urban-industrialized life', *Current Anthropology* 25: 346–347.

Hinsie, L. and Campbell, R. (1970) *Psychiatric Dictionary*, 4th edition, London: Oxford University Press.

Holton, R. (1985) *The Transition from Feudalism to Capitalism*, New York: St Martin's Press.

Horkheimer, M. and Adorno, T. (1982) [1948] *Dialectic of Enlightenment*, New York: Continuum.

Horowitz, I. (1976) 'Personality and structural dimensions in comparative international development', in C. Black (ed.) *Comparative Modernization*, New York: Free Press, pp. 257–277.

Ingram, D. (1987) *Habermas and the Dialectic of Reason*, New Haven: Yale University Press.

Inkeles, A. (1983) *Exploring Individual Modernity*, New York: Columbia University Press.

Inkeles, A. and Smith, D. (1974) *Becoming Modern*, Cambridge: Harvard University Press.

Institute of Social Research (1936) *Studien über Autorität und Familie*, Paris: Feliz Alcan.

Jackson, M. (1984) *Self-esteem and Meaning*, Albany: SUNY Press.

Jacoby, R. (1975) *Social Amnesia*, Boston: Beacon.

Jameson, F. (1990) *Late Marxism: Adorno, or the Persistence of the Dialectic*, London: Verso.

Jay, M. (1973) *The Dialectical Imagination: A History of the Frankfurt School and the Institute of Social Research, 1923–1950*, Boston: Little, Brown.

—— (1984) *Adorno*, Cambridge, MA: Harvard University Press.

Jones, E. (1981) 'Critique of empathic science: on Kohut and narcissism', *Psychology and Social Theory* No. 2: 19–42.

Kaës, R. (1980) *L'idéologie: Etudes Psychoanalytiques*, Paris: Dunod.

Kardiner, A. (1945) *The Psychological Frontiers of Society*, New York: Columbia University Press.

Karnoouh, C. (1984) 'Culture and development', *Telos* 17(3): 71–82.

Kernberg, O. (1975) *Borderline Conditions and Pathological Narcissism*, New York: Jason Aronson.

—— (1977) *Object Relations Theory and Clinical Psychoanalysis*, New York: Jason Aronson.

—— (1985) *Internal World and External Reality*, New York: Jason Aronson.

Klein, M. (1935) 'A contribution to the psychogenesis of manic-depressive states', *International Journal of Psycho-Analysis* 16: 145–174.

Kodai, M. (1984) *Libido Illimited: Freud Apolitique?*, Paris: Points hors Ligne.

Kohli, M. (1986) 'Gesellschaftzeit und Lebenszeit: Der Lebenslauf im Struktur-wandel der Moderne', *Soziale Welt* 4: 183–208.
Kolakowski, L. (1990) *Modernity on Endless Trial*, Chicago: University of Chicago Press.
Kolb, D. (1986) *The Critique of Pure Modernity: Hegel, Heidegger, and After*, Chicago: University of Chicago Press.
Kovel, J. (1981) *The Age of Desire*, New York: Pantheon.
—— (1988) *The Radical Spirit*, London: Free Association.
Kroll, J. (1988) *The Challenge of the Borderline Patient*, New York: Norton.
Kuzmics, H. (1984) 'Elias' theory of civilization', *Telos* 17(3): 83–99.
Lacan, J. (1977) [1966] *Ecrits: a Selection*, New York: Norton.
Laclau, E. and Mouffe, C. (1985) *Hegemony and Socialist Strategy: Toward a Radical Democratic Politics*, London: Verso.
Lasch, C. (1977) *Haven in a Heartless World*, New York: Basic Books.
—— (1979) *The Culture of Narcissism*, New York: Norton.
Lefebvre, H. (1984) *Everyday Life in the Modern World*, New Brunswick: Trans-action.
Lerner, D. (1958) *The Passing of Traditional Society: Modernizing the Middle East*, Glencoe, IL: Free Press.
Lichtman, R. (1982) *The Production of Desire*, New York: Free Press.
Lindstrom, L. (1993) *Cargo Cult: Strange Stories of Desire from Melanesia and Beyond*, Honolulu: University of Hawaii Press.
Livesay, J. (1985) 'Habermas, narcissism, and status', *Telos* 18(2): 75–90.
Lorenzer, A. (1976) 'Symbols and stereotypes', in P. Connerton (ed.) *Critical Sociology*, New York: Penguin, pp. 134–152.
Luke, T. (1989) *Screens of Power*, Urbana: University of Illinois Press.
—— (1991) 'Community and ecology', *Telos* 24(2): 69–79.
Luke, T. W. and White, S. K. (1985) 'Critical theory, the information revolution, and an ecological path to modernity', in J. Forester (ed.) *Critical Theory and Public Life*, Cambridge: MIT Press, pp. 22–53.
Lummis, C. (1991) 'Development against democracy', *Alternatives* 16: 31–36.
MacCannell, D. (1976) *The Tourist: A New Theory of the Leisure Class*, New York: Schocken.
Marcuse, H. (1962) *Eros and Civilization*, New York: Vintage.
—— (1964) *One-dimensional Man*, Boston: Beacon.
—— (1969) *Essay on Liberation*, Boston: Beacon.
—— (1970) *Five Lectures: Psychoanalysis, Politics, and Utopia*, Boston: Beacon.
—— (1978) *The Aesthetic Dimension: Toward a Critique of Marxist Aesthetics*, Boston: Beacon.
Marks, J. (1983) *Science and the Making of the Modern World*, London: Heinemann.
Marsella, A. (1978) 'The modernization of traditional cultures: consequences for the individual', in D. Hoopes, P. Pedersen, and G. Renwick (eds) *Overview of Intercultural Education, Training, and Research*, Vol. 3, La Grange Park, IL: Intercultural Network, pp. 108–147.
Martín-Baró, I. (1994) *Writings for a Psychology of Liberation Psychology*, Cambridge: Harvard University Press.
Mattelart, A. (1983) *Transnationals and the Third World*, South Hadley, MA: Bergin and Garvey.
Miller, A. (1986) 'Depression and grandiosity as related forms of narcissistic disturbances', in A. Morrison (ed.) *Essential Papers on Narcissism*, New York: NYU Press, pp. 323–347.

Miller, J. (1993) *The Passion of Michel Foucault*, New York: Simon and Schuster.

Mirowsky, J. (1989) *Social Causes of Psychological Distress*, New York: Aldine de Gruyter.

Mommsen, W. (1987) 'Personal conduct and societal change: toward a reconstruction of Max Weber's concept of history', in S. Lash and S. Whimster (eds) *Max Weber, Rationality, and Modernity*, London: Allen and Unwin, pp. 35–51.

Nandy, A. (1987) *Traditions, Tyranny and Utopia*, Delhi: Oxford University Press.

Narr, W.-D. (1985) 'Toward a society of conditioned reflexes', in J. Habermas (ed.) *Observations on 'The Spiritual Situation of the Age'*, Cambridge, MA: MIT Press, pp. 31–66.

Nash, M. (1984) *Unfinished Agenda: The Dynamics of Modernization in Developing Nations*, Boulder: Westview.

Naumann, J. and Hufner, K. (1985) 'Evolutionary aspects of social and individual development', in J. R. Nesselroade and A. von Eye (eds) *Individual Development and Social Change: Explanatory Analysis*, Orlando, FL: Academic Press, pp. 51–93.

O'Neill, J. (1985) 'Decolonization and the ideal speech community', in J. Forester (ed.) *Critical Theory and Public Life*, Cambridge: MIT Press, pp. 57–75.

Poggie, J. and Lynch, R. (eds) (1974) *Rethinking Modernization*, Westport, Conn: Greenwood.

Politzer, G. (1947) *La Crise de la Psychologie Contemporaine*, Paris: Editions Sociales.

Poole, R. (1991) *Morality and Modernity*, London: Routledge.

Poster, M. (1978) *Critical Theory of the Family*, New York: Seabury.

—— (1990) *The Mode of Information: Poststructuralism and Social Context*, Chicago: University of Chicago Press.

Rabinow, P. (ed.) (1984) *The Foucault Reader*, New York: Pantheon.

Robinson, P. (1969) *The Freudian Left*, New York: Harper and Row.

Rogers, E. (1969) *Modernization among Peasants*, New York: Holt, Rinehart and Winston.

Routledge, P. (1987) 'Modernity as a vision of conquest: development and culture in India', *Cultural Survival Quarterly* 11(3): 63–66.

Schafer, R. (1976) *A New Language for Psychoanalysis*, New Haven: Yale University Press.

Schmid, M. (1982) 'Habermas's theory of social evolution', in J. Thompson and D. Held (eds) *Habermas: Critical Debates*, Cambridge, MA: MIT Press, pp. 162–180.

Schneider, M. (1975) *Neurosis and Civilization: A Marxist-Freudian Synthesis*, New York: Seabury.

Sennett, R. and Cobb, J. (1973) *The Hidden Injuries of Class*, New York: Vintage.

Shapiro, D. (1965) *Neurotic Styles*, New York: Norton.

Simmel, G. (1971) [1903] 'The metropolis and mental life', in *On Individuality and Social Forms*, Chicago: University of Chicago Press, pp. 324–339.

Sloan, S. T. (1987) *Deciding: Self-deception in Life Choices*, London: Methuen.

—— (1990) 'Psychology for the Third World?', *Journal of Social Issues* 46(3): 1–20.

Snell, B. (1960) *The Discovery of the Mind*, New York: Harper and Row.

Stewart, A. and Healy, J. (1989) 'Linking individual development and social changes', *American Psychologist* 44(1): 30–42.

Stout, J. (1991) 'Modernity without essence', *Soundings* 74(3–4): 525–540.

Strasser, H. (ed.) (1981) *An Introduction to Theories of Social Change*, London: Routledge and Kegan Paul.

Stromberg, P. (1992) *Language and Self-transformation: A Study of the Christian Conversion Narrative*, New York: Cambridge University Press.

Thompson, E. P. (1963) *The Making of the English Working Class*, New York: Vintage.

Thompson, J. (1984) *Studies in the Theory of Ideology*, Berkeley: University of California Press.

Thomson, I. (1989) 'The transformation of the social bond: images of individualism in the 1920s versus the 1970s', *Social Forces* 67(4): 851–870.

Todd, E. (1987) *The Causes of Progress: Culture, Authority and Change*, New York: Basil Blackwell.

Tolman, C. (1994) *Psychology, Society, and Subjectivity: An Introduction to German Critical Psychology*, London: Routledge.

Tolman, C. and Maiers, W. (eds) (1991) *Critical Psychology: Contributions to a Historical Science of the Subject*, New York: Cambridge University Press.

Trainer, F. (1989) 'Reconstructing radical development theory', *Alternatives* 14: 481–515.

van Nieuwenhuijze, C. (ed.) (1984) *Development Regardless of Culture*, Leiden: E. J. Brill.

Wachtel, P. (1989) *The Poverty of Affluence: A Psychological Portrait of the American Way of Life*, Philadelphia: New Society.

Watson, L. (1970) 'Urbanization and the Guajiro matrifocal family: consequences for socialization and personality development', *Anthropologica* 27: 3–23.

Weber, M. (1958) *The Protestant Ethic and the Spirit of Capitalism*, New York: Scribners.

Westen, D. (1985) *Self and Society*, New York: Cambridge University Press.

Wexler, P. (1983) *Critical Social Psychology*, Boston: Routledge and Kegan Paul.

White, S. (1988) *The Recent Work of Jürgen Habermas*, New York: Cambridge University Press.

Whitebook, J. (1985) 'Reason and happiness: some psychoanalytic themes in critical theory', in R. Bernstein (ed.) *Habermas and Modernity*, Cambridge: MIT Press, pp. 140–160.

Wiersma, J. (1988) 'The press release: symbolic communication in life history interviewing', *Journal of Personality* 56(1): 205–238.

Wilensky, H. and Lebeaux, C. (1965) *Industrial Society and Social Welfare*, New York: Free Press.

Yeh, E.-K. (1985) 'Sociocultural changes and the prevalence of mental disorders in Taiwan', in W.-S. Tseng and D. Wu (eds) *Chinese Culture and Mental Health*, Orlando, FL: Academic Press, pp. 265–286.

Zaretsky, E. (1976) *Capitalism, the Family, and Personal Life*, New York: Harper and Row.

Zizek, S. (1989) *The Sublime Object of Ideology*, London: Verso.

—— (1991) *For They Know Not What They Do: Enjoyment as a Political Factor*, London: Verso.

Index

ideological formation 102–104, 107, 127
ideological reification 145; *see also* de-ideologization
individual and capitalism 101; and de-ideologization 108–109; and modernity 30–34
industrialization 34–38, 83; Marxist-Freudian critique 42, 45–46; and rationalization of production 51–53
Ingram, D. 50, 62
Inkeles, A. 29–34, 40, 88
insecurity 99
instinctual drives 87
interaction paradigms 75–76

Kernberg, O. 71, 75, 79, 88, 115
Klein, M. 78
Kohlberg 63, 106

Lacan, J. 71–72, 106
lifeworld 99, 122; colonization of 62–65, 110, 117, 119–120, 129; decolonization of 130–146; defined 50; of the infant 71; rationalization of 120; structural components 53–56; and system 135; *see also* symbolic
Livesay, J. 121–126
Lorenzer, A. 75, 113–115
Luke, T.W. 63–65, 90–92, 144, 142

Marcuse, H. 50, 82–89, 92, 132
Marsella, A. 15
Martín-Baró, I. 104, 142
Marx, K. 14, 56, 62; notion of ideology 102; his social theory and psychoanalytic theory 81
meaning 53; construction of 110
meaningfulness 63, 77, 110–113
meaninglessness 13, 63, 123, 129
mental health 23
mental illness 67
modernity 1, 127; characterized by change 9; and modern living 3–5; and personality theories 67; psychological impact 54–66; scholarly definitions 14–18
modernization 20–22; affirmative perspective 47; capitalist 114, 124, 128, 145; and consciousness 38–41; countermodernization movements 143; critical perspective 48; liberal

position 49; psychological consequences 24–26, 96
modern psyche, crisis of 23
mythical orientation *see* worldview

narcissism 115–117, 122, 124–126; *see also* depression
neo-Marxists 100, 109
neurosis 44–45, 103
nuclear family *see* bourgeois father

object relations 86, 93–94, 111–113, 122–123, 131
Oedipus complex 93, 119–120

performance principle 84, 120
personality 53, 130; and capacity for relatedness 77; style 73, 127
Piaget 59
pleasure principle 86
Poggie, J. and Lynch, R. 29
Poole, R. 132
Poster, M. 89–90, 137
postmodernists 100, 109, 136
pre-modern *see* worldview
privatization 98
Protestant ethic, and personality 60–61
psyche, crisis of 23; definition of 68; modern 83, 96, 105; personal style 73; structuring of 68–76, 114, 131
psychodynamic psychology 68; and Marxist social theory 81
psychologism 2
psychopathology, and class 89

radical democracy 144
rationality, aesthetic-expressive 87; cognitive instrumental 56–57, 59, 83, 114
redistribution of wealth 141–142
reflection 99
repressive desublimation 84

Schneider, M. 42–45
self–other differentiation 78–79; *see also* de-idealization and object relations
sociology 14
social context 1; and psychoanalysis 24
stereotypes 113–115, 131; *see also* ideology
subjectivity 68, 83; inter- 101, 131, 143